Praise for
The Smartest Investment Book You'll Ever Read

"Extremely solid advice … [Solin's] recommendations
are sound and simple to put into effect."
—*The New York Times*

"Bay Street will hate this indexing manifesto
that urges Canadians to dump their advisors
and go global in their investments."
—Jonathan Chevreau, *National Post*
personal finance columnist

"An investor who reads nothing else would have good guidance
and maybe handsome returns based on Solin's advice."
—Andrew Allentuck, author of *Bonds for Canadians:
How to Build Wealth and Lower Risk in Your Portfolio*
and contributor to *The Globe and Mail*

"*The Smartest Investment Book You'll Ever Read* will provide
the enlightenment and the gumption to free yourself from the
clutches of the investment industry and the wisdom and
direction necessary to get yourself back on track."
—William J. Bernstein, author of *The Intelligent Asset
Allocator* and *The Four Pillars of Investing*

"Dan Solin brings a unique perspective to the obstacles individuals often confront in achieving rates of return that should be theirs for the taking. Anyone applying his simple but powerful message will enhance their chances of investment success."

—Weston J. Wellington, vice-president
Dimensional Fund Advisors

Praise for
Does Your Broker Owe You Money?

"A candid look at the business of buying investment advice. Believe me, it isn't pretty."
—Jonathan Clements, *The Wall Street Journal*

"Solin's writing is clear…. His legal background offers a perspective rarely found in investment books."
—*BetterInvesting Magazine*

"[A] bold new book."
—*The San Diego Union-Tribune*

"Enable[s] the average investor to avoid being victimized…. This book is required reading for all brokerage house clients."
—William J. Bernstein, author of *The Intelligent Asset Allocator* and *The Four Pillars of Investing*

The Smartest
Investment
Book
You'll Ever Read

Also by Daniel R. Solin

Does Your Broker Owe You Money?

The Smartest Investment Book

You'll Ever Read

The Simple, Stress-Free Way to Reach Your Investment Goals

Daniel R. Solin

VIKING
CANADA

VIKING CANADA

Published by the Penguin Group

Penguin Group (Canada), 90 Eglinton Avenue East, Suite 700, Toronto, Ontario, Canada   M4P 2Y3
(a division of Pearson Canada Inc.)

Penguin Group (USA) Inc., 375 Hudson Street, New York, New York 10014, U.S.A.
Penguin Books Ltd, 80 Strand, London WC2R 0RL, England
Penguin Ireland, 25 St Stephen's Green, Dublin 2, Ireland (a division of Penguin Books Ltd)
Penguin Group (Australia), 250 Camberwell Road, Camberwell, Victoria 3124, Australia
(a division of Pearson Australia Group Pty Ltd)
Penguin Books India Pvt Ltd, 11 Community Centre, Panchsheel Park, New Delhi – 110 017, India
Penguin Group (NZ), cnr Airborne and Rosedale Roads, Albany, Auckland 1310, New Zealand
(a division of Pearson New Zealand Ltd)
Penguin Books (South Africa) (Pty) Ltd, 24 Sturdee Avenue, Rosebank, Johannesburg 2196, South Africa

Penguin Books Ltd, Registered Offices: 80 Strand, London WC2R 0RL, England

Published in Canada by Viking Canada, a division of Pearson Canada Inc., 2006
Published in the United States by Perigee Books, a division of Penguin Group (U.S.A.) Inc., 2006

1   2   3   4   5   6   7   8   9   10   (RRD)

Manufactured in the U.S.A.

ISBN-10: 0-670-06626-5
ISBN-13: 978-0-670-06626-1

Library and Archives Canada Cataloguing in Publication data available upon request
American Library of Congress Cataloging in Publication data available

Visit the Penguin Group (Canada) website at **www.penguin.ca**

Special and corporate bulk purchase rates available; please see
www.penguin.ca/corporatesales or call 1-800-810-3104, ext. 477 or 474

To hard-working Canadian investors: There is a better, easier, less stressful way to achieve your financial goals. I hope that the time you spend reading this book will be the best investment you will ever make.

Contents

Part Three
Smart Investors Know Better   **103**

Part Four
The Real Way Smart Investors
Beat 95% of the "Pros"   **117**

Introduction:
We Are Different,
but We Are the Same

With understandable pride, Canadians celebrate their differences from their American neighbours. However, when it comes to investing, the two countries are remarkably the same.

- Actively managed mutual funds in both countries are aggressively marketed.
- Active managers in Canada have the same dismal record as their American counterparts at beating an unmanaged index of stocks, while charging higher fees for this underperformance.
- Hedge funds and other "alternative" investments are poorly understood in both countries, leading investors to assume risks that they neither understand nor can afford to take.
- Investors in both countries are under the mistaken belief that investing is extremely complex and difficult, requiring the services of brokers and advisors to provide the necessary guidance.
- The brokers and advisors to whom investors turn for advice in both countries are conflicted and often poorly trained in basic principles of finance. As a consequence, they often do more harm than good.

The reality is that investing is quite simple and easy. The vast majority of investors do not need any advice or guidance from so-called investment professionals. Instead, in less than 90 minutes a year, most investors can select one of four basic portfolios and, based on historical returns, are likely to beat the returns achieved by 95% or more of professional money managers.

Let me state it very bluntly: The road to financial perdition begins with the call to your broker or financial advisor who tells you he or she can "beat the markets."

Canadians would be far better off if they took control of their own finances and never dealt with any broker or advisor.

PART ONE

Become a Smart Investor: Change Your Investment Life Forever

Chapter 1

An Unbelievable Chimp Story

*The investor's chief problem—and even his worst enemy—
is likely to be himself.*
—Benjamin Graham, *The Intelligent Investor*

There is a chimpanzee in a remote region of Sierra Leone that routinely performs open-heart surgery. His success rate is higher—and his mortality rate lower—than many of the finest heart surgeons in the world.

Okay, I made that up.

But, if you read that report in the newspaper, you would think that either

1. that chimp is really extraordinary; or
2. those heart surgeons are not very good.

If the story were true, and you needed a heart operation, you might seek out the chimp and avoid the heart surgeons.

The *Financial Times* of London annually runs a contest, pitting a neophyte investor against market analysts. In 2002, a five-year-old London girl chose stocks randomly from 100 pieces of paper listing companies on the *Financial Times* Stock Exchange. Her results were compared with those of a top financial analyst and those of a woman who used the "movement of the planets" to choose her portfolio.

Over a period of one year, the little girl won handily. Very handily, as a matter of fact. Her stocks gained 5.8%. In stark contrast, the portfolio of the professional analyst lost 46.2%. The analyst was also bested by the financial astrologer, whose stocks lost only 6.2%.

The little girl celebrated by going to McDonald's. I suspect the analyst continued to dine at more expensive establishments.

There are some excellent peer-reviewed studies that demonstrate that the stocks most highly rated by financial analysts consistently *underperform* the market.

Those reports are fact.

Either the little girl is very good, the analysts are very bad or the much-touted skill of stock picking is not something that any smart investor would want to bet the farm on.

And the chimp? Well, he still doesn't perform open-heart surgery.

Chapter 2

An Unbelievable True Story

Most individual investors would be better off in an index mutual fund.
—Peter Lynch, former manager of the Fidelity Magellan Fund, *Barron's,* April 2, 1990, p. 15

More than 50 million Canadian investors hold a total of more than $550 billion in mutual funds. Most of this money, and virtually all money held in individual stocks or in income trusts, is invested the *wrong* way—by **money managers** who engage in what I call "hyperactive management." Hyperactive management is characterized by efforts to beat the market by picking winners and timing the market. **This is dumb money**.

> **MONEY MANAGERS** are professionals who invest money on behalf of others. They take funds from individuals, pension funds, foundations and other endowments and invest it in markets according to particular criteria. Money managers are usually paid based on a percentage of the total money they invest. Therefore, if their investments make money and the pool of money they invest grows, so does their income.

In sharp contrast, *trillions* of dollars of assets of pensions, foundations and university endowments in Canada and the United States are invested the *right* way—by money managers who seek market returns by investing in all of the stocks and bonds in broad market indexes. **This is smart money**.

Ironically, investing for market returns—being among the smart money—is much easier than investing hyperactively.

- You don't have to pay any attention to the financial media.
- You don't have to sift though mountains of often-conflicting and confusing information from self-styled experts.
- It is less expensive.
- The results are demonstrably superior.
- The vast majority of Canadian investors do not need the advice of *any* advisor or broker.
- It should take you only 90 minutes or so a year.

Why then does such a gap exist between the investing strategy of smart money and the way most individual investors invest? This is because most investors use financial consultants employed by the major brokerage firms, banks or independent financial advisors who earn commissions or fees for selling financial products.

Virtually all of these brokerage-based financial consultants and most independent financial advisors manage money using dumb-money management techniques. They engage in **market timing** and **stock picking** because doing so makes them money.

> **MARKET TIMING** refers to the supposed ability to forecast whether the market is at a peak or in a valley, and to profit from that prediction.

> **STOCK PICKING** refers to the supposed ability to select stocks that are undervalued and will outperform the market over some future period of time.

The Truth about Dumb-Money Investing

Most financial advisors who work within this dumb-money system believe they have the ability to choose stocks and mutual funds that will outperform most other stocks and mutual funds—at least, that is what they tell their clients.

Or, if they admit they can't time the market and pick stocks, they tell their clients they can put their money with a money manager who *can* do these things.

But there is little independent, peer-reviewed, scientifically valid evidence that anyone can successfully engage in either market timing or stock picking consistently over the long term. In fact, all the evidence concludes that the opposite is true. To be sure, every year some managers do "beat the market" by beating their benchmark index. A few managers even do it for many years in a row. But the number of managers who beat the market is the number one would expect given statistical probability. The fact that these managers beat the market is not proof that they are better at what they do than others are. They beat the market because of simple chance.

Financial consultants, money managers and mutual fund managers who attempt to beat the market are engaged in hyperactive management. I call these investment professionals "hyperactive brokers and advisors" because that is what they are.

Smart-money investors avoid those advisors and money managers. They invest directly with **index fund** managers or in **Exchange Traded Funds** (ETFs). They know that, absent a lucky streak, the market return is really the best return.

INDEX FUNDS are mutual funds (pools of money from many small investors) that invest in all or a substantial number of the stocks or bonds that comprise a particular index. Index funds are often referred to as "passive investments" because their managers do not buy and sell securities in an effort to earn more than the return on the index.

EXCHANGE TRADED FUNDS are index funds that trade on stock market exchanges.

You should invest this way, too—for market returns.

If you ignore this advice, you are doing yourself a huge disservice. The **securities industry** adds costs. It subtracts value. Advisors who counsel their clients that they can beat the markets are assured of success in one area: transferring money from their clients' pockets to their own.

The **SECURITIES INDUSTRY** is made up of the broker-age firms, investment banks, insurance companies and others entities that develop, package and market stocks and bonds in order for corporations and government entities to raise capital from outside investors and for investors to seek investment returns.

Why Hyperactive Management Is So Expensive

The biggest problem with hyperactive management is expenses. They are so substantial that, when coupled with taxes and other hidden costs, the odds of a hyperactively managed portfolio beating the comparable market returns over an extended period are very, very long.

The success of hyperactive brokers and advisors is really not success in investing, but *success in selling*. Their success in selling is based on five sacred beliefs, all of which are untrue.

1. Hyperactive brokers and advisors can beat the markets.
2. Hyperactive brokers and advisors can time the markets.
3. Market timing and stock selection are really important.
4. The more expensive a product or service, the more valuable it must be.
5. Things that are exclusive or elitist are more valuable.

Theirs is a system that depends on its ability to convince you, through the expenditure of hundreds of millions of dollars of advertising, that you need to listen to these "experts." You don't. Smart Investors don't give their money to hyperactive brokers or advisors to do things that they can do better themselves.

Chapter 3

Smart Investing Takes Less Time Than Brunch

The first key to wisdom is defined, of course, as assiduous and frequent questioning.
—Pierre Abélard, 1079–1142. *Sic et Non,* translated by W.J. Lewis

So why is this the smartest investment book you'll ever read? Because it is simple. It is understandable. It doesn't beat around the bush and it doesn't pull punches. It tells you exactly why you should call your stock-picking, market-timing, stock-broker or investment advisor today and tell him or her you are taking control of your money.

You are moving your money where you can get superior long-term returns without the hassle and worry you currently have with your investments. You have seen the light—the light of investing for market returns.

If that isn't smart, I don't know what is.

Brokers and investment advisors cannot beat market returns over the long term.

They talk the talk, but they can't walk the walk.

There are hundreds of academic studies that demonstrate this fact conclusively.

If investors knew this, they wouldn't use these brokers or advisors. But the securities industry, assisted by the financial media, perpetuates the myth that they are able to beat the markets consistently over the long term, and they hide the data that demonstrates conclusively that this simply is not true.

Investors of all stripes lose billions of dollars a year because they don't understand that there is an easy, surefire way to achieve market returns without using brokers or investment advisors.

And achieving market returns is a big deal. That's because there is ample data indicating that, over the long term, simply achieving market returns will beat 95% of all professionally managed investment portfolios.

Now that I have told you this secret, I am going to explain how you can achieve market returns. It is simple, easy and not expensive.

It will take you only a relatively brief time to read this book. But it is an investment of time that can change your life.

Once you have read the book, it shouldn't take you more than 90 minutes to implement the advice I provide. And, after that, it shouldn't take you more than 90 minutes a year to make sure your investment portfolio continues to be structured the way you want it to be.

And you can do this yourself—you won't have to rely on the advice of a broker or advisor whose financial interests are in conflict with yours.

Now, if taking control of your financial life in 90 minutes a year isn't smart, I don't know what is.

Chapter 4

Drop Me to the Bottom Line!

More often (alas), the conclusions (supporting active management) can only be justified by assuming that the laws of arithmetic have been suspended for the convenience of those who choose to pursue careers as active managers.
—William F. Sharpe, Nobel laureate in economics, 1990.
"The Arithmetic of Active Management," *Financial Analysts Journal,* vol. 47, no. 1, January/February 1991

The chart on page 14 is the bottom line. When you look at it, keep in mind that the "low-risk" portfolio has the highest percentage of **bonds** and the "high-risk" portfolio has the highest percentage of **stocks**.

BONDS are debt instruments. When you buy a bond, you are lending money to a corporation or a government entity. You receive a steady interest payment in return for as long as you hold the bond. If you hold the bond to maturity, you receive the face value of the bond at the expiration. If you sell the bond in the open market, it may be worth more or less than face value, depending on the current interest rate of comparable bonds.

STOCKS are ownership interests (equity) in companies. After a company has paid all of its expenses for the year (including taxes and interest on debt), the remainder belongs to the owners. The total money left divided by the number of shares of stock outstanding is known as the earnings per share (EPS). This EPS can be reused by the company for growth or can be returned to stockholders, either as dividends or through a repurchase of the stock by the company. The price of a share of stock increases or decreases in relation to the value potential investors put on it when they analyze the company's prospects for continuing to earn more than the company's costs in the future.

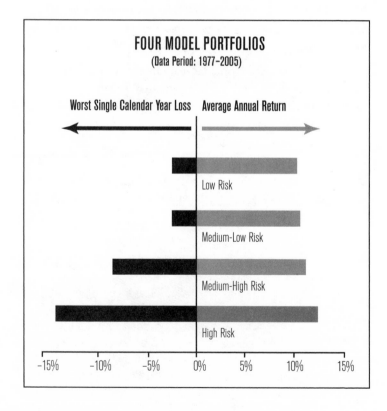

In less than a minute, you will understand the long-term historical returns and risks of the four portfolios that are suitable for the vast majority of investors. You can quickly compare the differences in returns and the differences in risk.

The following chart tells you the names of the ETFs, and the correct percentage of those ETFs, that you should purchase for the portfolio that you determine is the right one for you.

COMPOSITION OF FOUR MODEL PORTFOLIOS

FUND NAME	LOW RISK	MEDIUM- LOW RISK	MEDIUM- HIGH RISK	HIGH RISK
iShares CDN Composite Index Fund (XIC)	2%	4%	6%	8%
iShares CDN S&P 500 Index Fund (XSP)	10%	20%	30%	40%
iShares CDN MSCI EAFE Index Fund (XIN)	8%	16%	24%	32%
iShares CDN Bond Index Fund (XBB)	80%	60%	40%	20%
	100%	100%	100%	100%

These ETFs are all traded on the Toronto Stock Exchange. You can find more information about them at http://www.ishares.ca/index.do.

As I will explain, ETFs replicate the returns of all of the stocks in a specific segment of the market. For example, an S&P 500 ETF replicates the returns of the stocks of the 500 widely held companies that make up that index. In this way, without trying to time the market or pick a stock winner, this ETF will *always match the returns of the stocks of those 500 companies,* less the very low costs of the ETF and commissions incurred in buying it.

A **MARKET** is a mechanism by which potential buyers and potential sellers of items can be matched. In the world of stock and bond investments, some markets are physical while others exist only as computer-to-computer interchanges.

The overwhelming academic data indicates that investors who follow this advice will beat the returns of 95% or more of actively managed mutual funds over the long term.

No advice needed from brokers or advisors.

No worry. No stress.

But I know that some of you will not believe me. It just can't be this easy. You may even be skeptical about some of the data I discuss in this book. You can check the sources for all data by reading Chapter 43.

All I ask is that you read on with an open mind.

Chapter 5

Smart Investing Simply Makes Sense

If there are 10,000 people looking at the stocks and trying to pick winners, one in 10,000 is going to score, by chance alone, a great coup, and that's all that's going on. It's a game, it's a chance operation, and people think they are doing something purposeful ... but they're really not.
—Merton Miller, Nobel laureate in economics. Transcript of the PBS *Nova* special *The Trillion-Dollar Bet*, 2000

All parents understand the power of a name. That is why they often give their newborns names that reflect their aspirations or that connote the virtues they hope will become a part of their lives. Indeed, in ancient China and Egypt, the name of the emperor was thought to have such mystical power that the populace was forbidden to utter it, upon pain of death.

Such is the power of a name.

Those of us who advise clients on how to invest for market returns find ourselves burdened with names that have negative connotations. The current terminology is a snore; it makes our readers' and our clients' eyes glaze over.

The current terminology for investing for market returns is "passive investing." What could be more boring? Do you want to be an active investor or a passive investor? No one wants to be passive; it implies you have no ability to have any influence on an outcome.

Another term historically used for market-return investment is "index-based investing"—another less-than-scintillating bit of verbiage.

Over the years, index-based or passive investing has come to be equated with being "average." And no one wants to be average. We all want to believe in the utopian Shangri-La described in James Hilton's novel *Lost Horizon,* where everything is perfect and no one is average.

That's why we listen to hyperactive brokers and advisors who say, "Why do you want your portfolio to be average? I can help you make your portfolio superior. Our analysts can find undervalued stocks for you. We can determine when the market is overbought or oversold and help you manage your portfolio to go into and out of the market to maximize your return." Sound familiar?

But, in reality, there is nothing passive or average about investing for market returns. Nothing could be farther from the truth. This nomenclature is outdated and unfortunate, and it needs to be abandoned.

Welcome to the new world of "Smart Investing." It is populated by "Smart Investors."

You should be a Smart Investor.

Smart Investing is very simple. In a Smart Investment portfolio, you hold investments in a group of ETFs that, in turn, replicate the returns in all the securities (stocks or bonds) in a particular index. This portfolio is very easy to implement.

You will hold investments in funds that represent four broad indexes. The four types of index funds you will hold are

1. an index fund representative of the U.S. stock market in its broadest terms;
2. an index fund representative of the Canadian stock market in its broadest terms;
3. an index fund representative of the international stock market (exclusive of the U.S. and Canadian markets) in its broadest terms; and
4. an index fund representative of the Canadian bond market in its broadest terms.

I will show you how to determine the exact percentage of your portfolio that you will hold in each of these ETFs in greater detail later.

Smart Investing is, in reality, extremely aggressive, intelligent and very rewarding. It is based on academically verifiable data and quantitative risk management.

This data shows clearly and unmistakably that, over the long term, Smart Investors will consistently outperform those who attempt to beat the markets. That's not average; that's superior.

Conversely, investing with the goal of beating the markets is an ill-defined art, not a science. It is characterized by a lack of risk measurement. It is akin to financial astrology. It is, in many ways, the equivalent to gambling at a casino.

I call that approach "Hyperactive Investing." "Hyperactive Investors" listen to brokers and other financial advisors spin their tales of how one particular stock or another will somehow defy the logic of market efficiency, of how the whole world is wrong but that broker is right and the stock is not currently priced correctly. If you truly believe in markets, you believe that the market does, by definition, price each and every stock correctly as determined by buyers willing to buy at any given price and sellers willing to sell at any given price.

It is an easy choice: Smart Investing, based on reams of sound academic data that is easily verifiable, or Hyperactive Investing, based on hype and hope?

You may be surprised to learn that, according to a recent study, Smart Investing accounts for the vast majority of the trades in the United States. Unfortunately, it is likely that you, your friends and your neighbours are part of the disadvantaged minority if you are relying on the advice of your hyperactive broker or advisor.

And another comprehensive study of over 4000 mutual funds found that investors who selected mutual funds on their own *outperformed* the returns of mutual funds sold by brokers. And the difference was not trivial. It amounted to US$8.8 billion!

What does this important study demonstrate? Brokers and advisors are *harmful* to your financial well-being. You would be far better off investing yourself, for market returns.

Clearly, it's time to become a Smart Investor.

PART TWO

Your Broker or Advisor Is Keeping You from Being a Smart Investor

Chapter 6

Brokers Make Money When They Are Hyperactive

Q: "So investors shouldn't delude themselves about beating the market?"

A: "They're just not going to do it. It's just not going to happen."

—Daniel Kahneman, Nobel laureate in economics, 2002. Interview reported in the *Orange County Register*, January 2, 2002

Virtually all actively managed funds have, as a goal, beating a **benchmark index**. For example, many Canadian mutual funds have as their benchmark index the goal of beating the **S&P/TSX Composite Index**.

A **BENCHMARK INDEX** is an index that mutual funds use to measure their investment performance against the returns of a particular sector of the market for the purpose of comparison. The best-known benchmark index is the Standard and Poor's 500 Index, the index of 500 of the largest American companies by market capitalization. Mutual funds that invest in U.S. large-capitalization stocks typically use the S&P 500 Index as their benchmark.

The **S&P/TSX COMPOSITE INDEX** is the primary gauge for the market activity of Canadian-based stocks listed on the Toronto Stock Exchange.

Clearly, these funds provide no value to investors—or even provide a *negative* value—if they cannot beat their designated indexes, because investors could assure themselves of achieving the returns of the index—every year—by simply investing on their own in an index fund that holds all of the stocks in that index or in ETFs that replicate the returns of those stocks.

Therefore, it is of great significance (and a deep, dark secret rarely discussed by hyperactive brokers and advisors), that in excess of 90% of actively managed mutual funds in both Canada and the United States *fail* to equal or beat their benchmark indexes over the long term.

Indeed, you can look at any meaningful time period and you will find that the majority of hyperactively managed funds in Canada fail to beat an unmanaged S&P/TSX Composite Index, even when it is their stated goal to do so.

Study after study shows that, over a long period, Smart Investors outperform Hyperactive Investors who attempt to beat the markets by either trading themselves or using hyperactive brokers or advisors.

Hyperactive Investors lead the pack in one category: stress. They are on a fool's errand and don't know it. They believe they must constantly monitor the markets and listen to the conflicting views of the financial pundits. When all this attention still results in underperformance or even cataclysmic losses, their stress level goes off the charts.

The reason for the dismal record of Hyperactive Investors is a combination of trading costs and management fees. Hyperactive Canadian mutual funds cost more (average fees of 2.5% per year versus fees of under 0.30% for most ETFs) and trade more. Trading increases costs. Increased costs, through fees and trading, make it exceedingly difficult for hyperactively managed funds to equal the performance of ETFs, and that is why most of them fail to do so.

Here is what the raw data tells us:

- Hyperactively managed funds significantly underperform the market over the long term.
- It is much less stressful to be a Smart Investor.
- It is much less expensive to be a Smart Investor.
- Most investors do not need the advice of any broker or advisor to be a Smart Investor.

Here is the bottom line: Smart Investors will fare significantly better than Hyperactive Investors over the long run.

Chapter 7

A Loser's Game

Even as Wall Street belittles your investment abilities, it also wants you to believe you can beat the stock-market averages. This, of course, is contradictory. But it is also entirely self-serving. The more you trade and the more you invest with active money managers, the more money the Street makes. Increasingly, some of the market's savviest investors have turned their back on this claptrap. They have given up on active managers who pursue market-beating returns and instead have bought market-tracking index funds. But Wall Street doesn't want you to buy index funds, because they aren't a particularly profitable product for the Street. Instead, Wall Street wants you to keep shooting for market-beating returns. That is why you should be suspicious when you hear talk of the supposed "stock picker's market."

—Jonathan Clements, *You've Lost It, Now What?*

The actual returns of Hyperactive Investors are even worse than you might think.

One telling study involving mutual fund investors in the United States demonstrated that the average hyperactively managed fund investor had an annualized return for the 20-year period from 1985 to 2004 of 3.7%, when the S&P 500 Index returned 13.2%. The investor would have done better with bank certificates of deposit!

Another study examined the actual shareholder returns in specific actively managed funds and compared them with the reported returns of those funds. In fund after fund, Hyperactive Investors significantly underperformed the reported returns. For example, for the period 1998 to 2001, the Fidelity Aggressive Growth Fund reported returns of 2.8%, but the average Hyperactive Investor in that fund had a *loss* of 24.1%.

There is no reason to believe that a study of Canadian mutual fund investors would not yield the same, dismal results.

If the average fund earned 13.2%, shouldn't the average investor in those funds also have earned 13.2%? She should, but she doesn't. That's because Hyperactive Investors chase hot-performing funds. These investors pour their money into mutual funds *after* periods of good performance, hoping for a repeat performance. They are often disappointed.

Stated differently, Hyperactive Investors buy and sell stocks and/or mutual funds frequently.

I ask you, what could be sillier than frequently buying and selling mutual funds?

Mutual funds were originally conceived on the idea that small investors should not be buying and selling individual stocks frequently because transaction costs would eat up any potential profit. Instead, small investors should pool their money into a mutual fund, where a "professional" money manager buys and sells the stocks for them, in large blocks, with much lower commissions than an individual investor could get. In this way, the investor can "buy and hold" a good mutual fund, and the fund manager can indulge his or her illusive goal of beating the markets through stock picking and market timing.

Nice theory.

But today hyperactive brokers and advisors often recommend that their clients sell old mutual funds and invest in the next "hot" fund. This way, these "investment professionals" can continue to generate sales commissions.

Remember this: The proof is overwhelming that Smart Investing—investing for market returns—outperforms attempting to beat the markets over the long term.

Why then is it so difficult to convince individual investors to be Smart Investors? There are a number of reasons, but the most compelling has to do with a marketing juggernaut of hyperactive brokers—paid for with money earned from their clients, no less.

Another equally important reason has to do with human psychology.

And yet a third has to do with what is called "financial pornography," the incessant blathering of financial writers and talking heads from the print press, television, the web and other media sources.

By the way, I know your time is valuable. So if at any time you feel convinced and don't want to read any more, you can skip right to Chapter 33, where I lay out a four-step process for taking control of your financial life and becoming a Smart Investor.

Chapter 8

Why Investors Pursue Hyperactive Investing

*Santa Claus and the Easter Bunny should take a few
pointers from the mutual-fund industry [and its fund
managers]. All three are trying to pull off elaborate hoaxes.
But while Santa and the bunny suffer the derision of eight-
year-olds everywhere, actively managed stock funds still
have an ardent following among otherwise clear-thinking
adults. This continued loyalty amazes me. Reams of statistics
prove that most of the fund industry's stock pickers fail to
beat the market. For instance, over the 10 years through
2001, U.S. stock funds returned 12.4% a year, vs. 12.9%
for the Standard & Poor's 500 stock index.*
—Jonathan Clements, "Only Fools Fall in … Managed
Funds?" *The Wall Street Journal,* September 15, 2002

The evidence that Smart Investing is superior to Hyperactive
Investing is both compelling and overwhelming. Yet in excess
of 90% of all *individual* investors continue to be Hyperactive
Investors.

Here are the primary reasons.

Marketing

Hyperactive brokers and advisors spend hundreds of millions of dollars on very slick marketing campaigns to push their services. Who can forget the television commercial where the broker assumes the role of father of the bride? Those of us who are old enough still remember John Houseman, the wonderful actor who played the law school professor in the film *The Paper Chase,* telling us that the company he represented "make(s) money the old-fashioned way, we earn it." And who doesn't remember the name of the brokerage firm for which everybody in the ad stops to listen when the broker from that firm whispers into his client's ear?

Guess where all the money comes from for these companies to create those marketing campaigns and buy those advertising pages and minutes? Of course: It comes from the commissions and other fees charged to those hapless Hyperactive Investors with the supposedly invaluable assistance of their hyperactive advisors.

How perfect is that? The firms that separate you from your money use a piece of that money to create more marketing and advertising material to get you and others to give them more money to invest—at lower returns than you can get from being a Smart Investor.

Kind of like digging your own grave before the firing squad mows you down.

Gambling

There is a well-documented psychological attraction to gambling activities; we all have this attraction to one degree or another. Some people indulge in "recreational" gambling at a casino. Others have a more profound attraction and gamble more frequently and for larger stakes than others.

One study of speculative investors in Ontario noted the possible linkage between these investors and problem gamblers.

Being a Hyperactive Investor fuels this psychological attraction. The fact that hyperactive brokers and advisors can produce intermittent "winners" reinforces this instinct, just like the sound of coins hitting the tray at a slot machine. But just as gamblers ultimately fall to the house at the casino, Hyperactive Investors will ultimately be the losers. The house in this case is the brokerage firm.

Desire to Seek Order

There is another well-documented human tendency—to find order where it does not exist, and thus to confuse luck with skill. The most commonly cited example is research showing that a basketball player with a "hot hand" is no more likely to make his next shot than at any other time. Shooting a basketball is essentially like a coin toss. Every shot is an independent event, and the chances of making it have to do more with how close the player is to the basket and how much pressure he or she is under than whether or not the player has made the last six shots.

In the financial world, the widespread use of so-called technical tools to predict the market is a perfect example of this desire for order. Technical analysis, which uses these technical tools, looks at patterns of stock prices (so-called charting) in an effort to divine the stock's next movement. There are exhaustive studies demonstrating that technical analysis has absolutely no validity, yet it continues to be used by many Hyperactive Investors and their brokers.

Overconfidence

People are overconfident of their own abilities. This is particularly true of men, whose perception of their skill in many areas—especially athletics—is often at odds with objective reality.

The vast majority of hyperactive brokers and advisors underperform the markets over the long term. Few will admit it, and most retain total confidence in their ability to beat the markets in the future. Or at least they appear to have this confidence, which is a very good sales tool.

Really, if your hyperactive broker or advisor told you the truth and said, "I have no idea where the markets are headed or which stocks are a good buy," would you use his or her services?

Looking for "Sizzle" (in All the Wrong Places)

A financial pundit recently noted that convincing people to invest for market returns has the same appeal as serving a vegetarian dinner at a cattlemen's convention. There is no "sizzle." No "double your money in six weeks." No complicated software to learn. No "hot" stock or mutual fund to select.

There is no rush that Hyperactive Investors get from that feeling of dealing with their hyperactive brokers on a constant basis and trying to outwit other investors. No bragging rights at the nineteenth hole as to what a great broker they have and how their broker picked a stock that "really took off." No need to even follow the financial pundits, much less engage in the kind of frenetic, counterproductive and obsessive attention to every new scrap of financial news generated by media, delivered breathlessly, minute by minute, throughout the day.

Understanding the reasons why investors ignore reality and continue to be Hyperactive Investors is very important.

It is significant that superior market performance is not one of them. To the contrary, Smart Investors have demonstrably superior returns over the long term.

You would think that this fact would carry the day.

Chapter 9

The "Activity" Myth

Properly measured, the average actively managed dollar must underperform the average passively managed dollar, net of costs.
—William F. Sharpe, Nobel laureate in economics, 1990. "The Arithmetic of Active Management," *Financial Analysts Journal,* vol. 47, no. 1, January/February 1991

Most people confuse activity with progress and passivity with lack of initiative. That is part of the problem with the current investing nomenclature.

With investing, activity is not progress. Activity is cost. And cost just eats up investment return.

A well-known study demonstrated that investors who engage in the most trading are the ones who most significantly underperform the market. The conclusion of the study was that "trading is hazardous to your wealth."

Hyperactive brokers and advisors, and especially online firms for do-it-yourself investors, encourage trading. They tell investors to sell stocks or funds that have underperformed in order to "get rid of dogs" and use the tax loss to offset gains on other trades. They encourage investors to buy the next "hot" stock or fund.

But study after study shows that all of this trading does only one thing for investors—it transfers money from their accounts to their hyperactive brokers' and advisors' pockets in the form of commissions and fees.

That is why Smart Investors generally fare better than Hyperactive Investors.

Chapter 10

What's Wrong with Hyperactive Investing?

Why does indexing outmanoeuvre the best minds on Wall Street? Paradoxically, it is because the best and brightest in the financial community have made the stock market very efficient. When information arises about individual stocks or the market as a whole, it gets reflected in stock prices without delay, making one stock as reasonably priced as another. Active managers who frequently shift from security to security actually detract from performance [compared to an index fund] by incurring transaction costs.
—Burton G. Malkiel, "Why the Critics Are Wrong,"
The Wall Street Journal Interactive Edition, May 24, 1999

What is wrong with trying to beat the markets?

Just about everything.

The corporate culture is troublesome. And many, if not most, of the hyperactive brokers and advisors who encourage their clients to be Hyperactive Investors (whether they are on Bay Street or Wall Street) are qualified only in sales, not in finance.

But the biggest problem with the Bay Street/Wall Street investing approach is that it is premised on a set of beliefs that have *no* credible support:

- Hyperactive brokers and advisors can time the market.
- Hyperactive brokers and advisors can pick stocks or mutual funds that will beat the market.
- Hyperactive brokers and advisors can pick fund managers who will beat the market.

In addition:

- The hyperactive investing system used by most brokers and financial advisors ignores the effects of fees, trading costs and other expenses, taxes and inflation, on the ultimate investment returns.
- The system is fraught with conflicts of interest, from broker compensation to the relationship between advertising and news in the financial media.
- The system often fails to measure risk, thereby exposing investors to portfolios that are far too risky, with terrible consequences.
- Many hyperactive brokers and advisors in this system have successfully avoided being held to a fiduciary standard because they know they cannot meet that standard in their relationships with investors.

In short, being a Hyperactive Investor is a fool's errand. It is a zero-sum game (or worse, when you consider transaction costs), except from the perspective of the hyperactive brokers and advisors.

They make out just fine.

Chapter 11

Brokers Aren't on Your Side

It [is] a fundamental dishonesty, a fundamental problem that cuts to the core of the lack of integrity on Wall Street.
—Eliot L. Spitzer, attorney general of New York. Interview on *NOW with Bill Moyers,* May 24, 2002

You need to have utmost trust, faith and confidence in your financial advisor and in the firm that employs him or her.

But there is unsettling news about advisors' integrity—or lack thereof. One study looked at the analyst ratings of 50 banking and brokerage firms in the United States as they related to 19 companies that went bankrupt in 2002. The study demonstrated that

1. 94% of the 50 firms continued to advise investors to buy or hold shares in the companies up to the date the companies filed for bankruptcy; and
2. 12 of the 19 companies continued to receive "buy" or "hold" ratings on the actual date they filed for bankruptcy.

In 2002, many of the best-known and most respected brokerage firms in the United States, which employ hordes of hyperactive brokers, entered into a $1.4-billion settlement (without admitting that they had done anything wrong!) to resolve allegations that they duped their clients by issuing misleading analyst reports.

If prominent brokerage firms filled with hyperactive brokers have no demonstrated ability to give accurate and reliable advice, and if you give credence to New York Attorney General Eliot Spitzer's observation about their "lack of integrity," why would you continue to rely on them for investment advice?

No advisor who advocates Smart Investing was the subject of any of these allegations. These advisors do not believe, employ or rely upon stock analysts.

Smart Investing advisors make no predictions about the future performance of the market as a whole or about any particular stock. Instead, they focus on **asset classes** (and their returns), **asset allocation, risk management** and a solid, academically based belief system that has consistently been demonstrated to outperform hyperactive brokers and advisors over the long term.

> **ASSET CLASSES** are the three major groupings under which financial assets fall: stocks, bonds and cash. Stocks are ownership shares in a company. Bonds are loans to a company or a government entity. Cash is not just currency, but also chequing and savings accounts held in banks and money market funds.

ASSET ALLOCATION is the way that asset classes are divided up in an investment portfolio. Depending on an individual investor's time horizon and tolerance for risk, he or she will allocate the money in the portfolio in different proportions among stocks, bonds and cash.

RISK MANAGEMENT refers to the techniques that can be used to reduce the risk of an investment portfolio. Risk is the measure of the probability of potential outcomes and the change in portfolio value that would occur if those outcomes came to pass.

Make proper asset allocation your new investment goal. Once you accept the premise that asset allocation is far more important than stock picking or market timing, your financial life will become a stress-free walk in the park and your money will start to grow.

Chapter 12

Hyperactive Brokers, Underachieving Students

[T]he majority of financial advisors are people who changed careers and who had no formal academic training in the field of financial advice.... [T]he prevailing culture is one of sales rather than one of professionalism.
—John J. De Goey's submission in response to Finance Canada's 2006 Review of Financial Sector Legislation. Reported at: http://www.fin.gc.ca/consultresp/06Rev_12e.html

Call me picky, but if I am going to entrust my life savings to an advisor (assuming that I need one at all; most Smart Investors don't), I want him or her to have a Ph.D. in finance, or comparable credentials, from a major university. After all, isn't knowledge of finance the critical qualification needed to give investment advice?

I don't have much regard for the credentials bandied about by hyperactive brokers and financial advisors. Titles like "vice-president, investments" are handed out like candy, and not on the basis of academic credentials, client service or even the performance of clients' portfolios. They are handed out on the basis of commissions and fees generated for the firm.

I wouldn't use any advisor, regardless of his or her qualifications, who tells me that he or she can beat the markets. But it is useful nonetheless for you as an investor to know something about real qualifications.

Only a small percentage of hyperactive brokers and advisors have credentials indicating that they have engaged in any serious study of finance. Instead, the focus of their training is on the financial products they will be selling, and it therefore emphasizes sales over knowledge of basic financial principles.

As I will explain later, the vast majority of Smart Investors do not need to spend money to seek the advice of *any* advisor. Instead, they should invest the money they would otherwise be paying an advisor in order to increase their total nest egg.

Chapter 13

What Do You Think of These Odds?

Exceptions aside, it's clear that many billion-dollar Canadian equity funds are just what you'd expect: overpriced index funds. They may lag the index and on occasion slightly beat it, but, by and large, they thrive or languish along with the index.

—Jonathan Chevreau, "Outing 'Closet' Index Funds," *Financial Post,* November 5, 2005. Reported at: http://www.canada.com/national/nationalpost/financialpost/ fpweekend/story.html?id=fc98997b-10cf-4b0b-9bb1- 5d900bf907bf

The next three chapters have to do with the inability of hyperactive brokers, advisors and investment managers to time the market or pick winners. Before that, I want to tell you about a study done in 2003 by my colleague and friend Edward S. O'Neal, Ph.D., an assistant professor of finance at the Babcock Graduate School of Management at Wake Forest University, which was published in my previous book, *Does Your Broker Owe You Money?* As I have stated, there are many academic studies that show that Hyperactive Investing is a fool's errand. I like O'Neal's study because it is so easy to understand.

First, he looked at the performance of all 494 actively managed mutual funds in the United States that had, as their goal, beating the S&P 500 Index for the five-year period July 1993 through June 1998.

How hard could this be? The managers of these funds are among the best, brightest and highest-paid people in this country. Some of them earn millions of dollars to beat the S&P. Their funds charge more than eight times the cost of a simple index fund, like the Vanguard 500 Index Fund (VFINX). And we know this fund will *always* give investors the returns of the S&P 500 Index (reduced only by the amount of its low fees), because it is set up to do precisely that.

O'Neal then did the same analysis for the next five-year period, from July 1998 through June 2003.

Here is what he found: Only 46% of the actively managed funds beat the index during the first five-year period and only a pathetic 8% beat the index during the second five-year period.

And here is the real kicker: How many of these funds beat the S&P 500 Index during *both* periods? In O'Neal's own words:

> These results are sad indeed. The number of funds that beat the market in both periods is a whopping 10—or only 2% of all large cap funds.

Here is O'Neal's bottom line. It should be yours as well:

> Investors, both individual and institutional, and particularly 401(k) [retirement] plans, would be far better served

by investing in passive or passively managed funds than in trying to pick more expensive active managers who purport to be able to beat the markets.

O'Neal's study also demonstrates that there is no relationship between a fund that performs well during one period and its performance during an ensuing period. This irrefutable fact makes the exercise of trying to pick a "winning" fund even more improbable.

Are the results any better for Canadian mutual funds? In order to answer this question, I looked at the performance of all 81 Canadian mutual funds that had a 15-year track record and had, as a goal, beating the S&P/TSX Composite Index. Only 17 of them (20.99%) were able to do so. And even this number is overstated because it does not include those funds that performed badly during this period and were no longer included in the database available to researchers.

There are a number of very comprehensive studies of Canadian mutual funds that reach precisely the same conclusion: Relatively few actively managed funds are able to consistently beat the S&P/TSX Composite Index.

Of course, you could try to be one of the lucky investors who picks one of the small percentage of actively managed Canadian mutual funds that beat the markets. Or you could confront statistical reality and common sense and invest in ETFs that will give you market returns 100% of the time.

By the way, don't expect to be richly rewarded even if you are lucky enough to invest in one of the actively managed funds that does beat the index. Most of the relatively few funds that beat the index do so by less than 1%. So where is the big payoff for paying a hefty premium to invest in a fund that has such a small likelihood of beating the index in the first place?

The choice seems obvious, but most investors, egged on by their hyperactive brokers and advisors, make the wrong one. They attempt to find a "hot" fund that will beat the markets, and suffer the inevitable costly consequences.

Smart Investors don't chase "hot" funds.

Chapter 14

Nobody Can Time the Market

But you know as well as I that there's simply no evidence that funds have been successful at market timing.
—Remarks by John C. Bogle, founder, the Vanguard Group, president, Bogle Financial Markets Research Center, to the Bullseye 2000 Conference, Toronto, Canada, December 4, 2000. Reported at: http://www.vanguard.com/bogle_site/december042000.html

If anyone could consistently time the market, you would think it would be the authors of market-timing newsletters. They charge investors for access to their tip sheets about when to move money into or out of particular markets. But a study of more than 15,000 predictions made by 237 U.S. market-timing newsletters between June 1980 and December 1992 demonstrated that 94.5% of the newsletters had *gone out of business,* with an average length of operation of about four years.

What if your broker was Alan Greenspan, the venerable former chairperson of the Federal Reserve Board? How lucky you are! Who in the world knows more about the direction of the markets than Alan Greenspan? After all, the Federal Reserve Bank sets monetary policy and is responsible for the stability of the financial system in the United States.

Alan calls you. He says he is worried that the market is overheated. He refers to the investor enthusiasm for stocks as "irrational exuberance." He is concerned about a meltdown similar to the one experienced in Japan in the early 1990s.

Would you listen to him and dump the stocks in your portfolio? I suspect you would. Well, Alan made such a prediction, in 1996. And if you had listened to him you would have missed out on a three-year stock-market boom where the S&P 500 doubled in value.

So much for Mr. Greenspan's ability to time the market.

Do you think your hyperactive broker or advisor has more reliable information than Alan Greenspan?

The reason neither Alan Greenspan nor your hyperactive broker or advisor can accurately predict the financial markets in Canada or the United States is that neither of them has the power to change the psychology of these markets. Alan Greenspan's comment about "irrational exuberance" was his attempt to use his position of influence to "talk the market down" from the dizzying heights it had begun to attain even early in what we know now in hindsight was a bubble.

Although his remarks caused a little downward blip, there was enough energy in the market to propel it upward for more than another three years. Any prediction that a financial market will go up or that it will go down is, at some point, going to prove right. The issue is when that time will be.

Those who adhere to market timing almost always miss the absolute top or the absolute bottom. They are either too early, like those who bailed out when Alan Greenspan first spoke of irrational exuberance. Or they are too late, like those who hung on through 2001 and 2002 after the stock market crashed and burned, because other stock market "experts" told them to use "dips in the market as buying opportunities." But creating the illusion of their ability to time the market is critical to the business of hyperactive brokers and advisors. After all, if they have this ability and you don't, you need to rely on their advice, which means you need to pay their fees. The only problem is that this is an expertise they don't have, because it is an expertise that does not exist.

Yet the talking heads on television and many hyperactive brokers and advisors are always talking about what is going to happen in the market, as if they actually have information upon which to make these prognostications.

They don't.

No one does.

Market timing, like stock picking (which I'll discuss in a little while) is nothing but a shell game. You should never listen to anyone who says he or she can time the market, no matter how qualified or confident that person appears to be.

Advisors to Smart Investors never rely on market timing. They understand that if Alan Greenspan can't do it, neither can they.

Smart Investors never engage in market timing because they know it is a sham.

Chapter 15

Nobody Can Consistently Beat the Market

Mutual funds have become an important part of the Canadian investors' savings. The value added by money managers on a long-term basis is meagre and inconsistent. For a holding period of five years or more, only a quarter of mutual funds outperform the market and a mere 5% of the funds consistently perform higher than the median returns.

—Study authored by Rajeeva Sinha, professor of finance, Odette School of Business, University of Windsor, and Vijay M. Jog, professor of finance, Eric Sprott School of Business, Carleton University, August 17, 2004

"Stock picking" refers to the ability to select stocks or mutual funds that will outperform the market.

Virtually all hyperactive brokers and advisors tell you they have the ability to engage in stock picking. After all, that is how they justify the fat fees and commissions they get paid.

Every actively managed mutual fund manager believes he or she has this ability.

Here's a true story, not like the story about the chimp that performs open-heart surgery.

After I published my previous book, *Does Your Broker Owe You Money?* I received telephone calls and emails from brokers and ex-brokers who told me stories that would make your skin crawl.

One of my favourites was told by a man who had left a job with a major brokerage firm in order to advise clients to invest for market returns. He told me about the training he had received a few years earlier when he started work at this major—and well-respected—brokerage firm. He and the other brokers in training were told to split their potential client list in half. They were told to call half and tell them to buy a particular stock. The other half were to receive calls telling them to sell the same stock.

In two weeks, these "financial advisor" trainees were told to note which way the stock had moved, up or down. Whichever way it had moved, half of the potential client list would think the trainee was pretty smart to be able to pick a stock like that.

They were told to split this "successful" half of their group again, and to do the same thing: Tell half that a stock would go up and half that the same stock would go down.

If they did this three times, and started with a call list of 120 potential clients, after three "successful stock picks" they should then have fifteen "warm leads," people who had enough confidence in their ability to pick stocks to become clients.

Talk about a shell game!

If anyone could successfully pick stocks, you would think it would be the much-touted analysts who work for the most prestigious Wall Street firms. After all, they spend all of their time studying companies, trying to glean information that will assist them in selecting stocks that will outperform the market. It is their work product that hyperactive brokers often use as the basis for recommendations to Hyperactive Investors.

However, many studies of analyst recommendations find little support for their ability to pick stock winners. These studies indicate that analysts are sometimes right and sometimes wrong. When analysts are wrong, it is the investors who rely on their supposed expertise who lose money.

For example, as one prominent study by Patrick Bajari and John Krainer noted, "[I]n 2000 and 2001, the least recommended stocks earned an average abnormal return of 13%, while the most highly recommended stocks earned average abnormal returns of –7%." Ouch!

Even studies that demonstrate that there can be value in analyst recommendations note that, in order to take advantage of them, such heavy trading is required that the transaction costs incurred essentially offset the benefits obtained by relying on these recommendations.

If this is true, it is difficult to understand what value these recommendations really have—even when they are correct.

Finally, given the number of analyst recommendations, and the conflicting studies about their reliability, how do Hyperactive Investors know which ones have value and which ones don't? Hyperactive Investing clearly is a crapshoot.

Unfortunately, as with market timing, there is no evidence that anyone can consistently engage in stock picking. And, as I'll explain later, it turns out that stock picking accounts for only a small minority of all of the trades in the U.S. markets, and that number is declining. Clearly, the message is getting out. Unfortunately, however, it has reached neither the vast majority of individual investors in Canada and the United States nor virtually all of the hyperactive brokers and advisors who give them "professional advice."

Smart Investors do not engage in stock picking. They know that it is a fool's errand.

Smart Investors are not fools.

Chapter 16

Nobody Can Pick "Hot" Fund Managers

[T]o be fair, I don't think that you'd want to pay much attention to Morningstar's star ratings either.
—John Rekenthaler, director of research, Morningstar, *In the Vanguard,* Autumn 2000

"Morningstar gives this fund its five-star rating!"

How many times have you heard that line from your hyperactive broker who is trying to convince you to buy a "hot" mutual fund?

It is a convincing pitch. After all, Morningstar is the industry leader in ranking mutual funds, using its "star" system. It would be hard to find anyone who does not agree that Morningstar has more data about mutual funds than anyone else in the world. Most people think that, with these vast resources, Morningstar could predict mutual funds that would outperform the markets.

Most people are wrong.

Morningstar rates mutual funds by giving them from one to five stars depending on their performance. A five-star rating indicates the best performing funds. Although Morningstar notes that its ratings system should not be used to predict future performance, many hyperactive brokers and advisors ignore this admonition.

An exhaustive study of the performance record of funds rated "five stars" by Morningstar failed to find reliable statistical evidence that these funds performed any better than funds rated four stars or even three stars. The study also found that Morningstar ratings did only marginally better than other, far more simplistic, predictors of future performance.

So much for the predictive ability of the "star" system.

If Morningstar can't do it, ask yourself whether you should listen to your hyperactive broker or advisor who claims that he or she can. No one has the ability to predict the next "hot" manager. All we know is that it is unlikely that he or she will be "hot" for long.

Hyperactive Investors typically hold a mutual fund in their portfolio for four years or less.

Why do they switch funds? After all, as I previously noted, the concept of a mutual fund was to allow small investors who didn't have time to research investments and pick their own stocks to "buy and hold" a fund and let the "investment professional" do the stock picking.

Hyperactive Investors switch funds because they are convinced by the financial media or by their hyperactive broker or advisor that they can do better in a "hot" mutual fund run by a "hot" mutual fund manager. And the coveted Morningstar five-star rating is frequently what convinces these investors to sell lower-rated funds and buy the newly designated ones rated "five stars."

Why do some hyperactive brokers misuse the Morningstar rating system in this manner? More trading means more commissions.

Unfortunately, it also means lower returns for the investor.

Smart Investors don't care who is "hot" and who is not. And they place no more value on Morningstar's "star" ratings than they do on the movement of the planets.

Chapter 17

Why Recommend This Mutual Fund?

"American Funds dressed up these arrangements with fancy names like 'execution revenue,' 'target commissions' or 'Broker Partnership Payments,'" said Lockyer. "But, when you look beneath the cloak of legitimacy, the payments are little more than kickbacks to buy preferential treatment. Investors deserve to know that. The law American Funds violated is based on that simple principle."

—California Attorney General Bill Lockyer, commenting on a securities fraud lawsuit filed against American Funds' Los Angeles–based distributor and investment manager. Press release dated March 23, 2005

There are literally thousands of mutual funds. Hyperactive brokers and advisors make recommendations every day about which one you and other investors should buy.

Most people think that, when a broker or financial advisor makes a mutual fund recommendation, the investor is receiving objective advice about funds that can beat the markets.

Of course, as we have seen, no one has the ability to select such funds with any consistency. But still, in any given year, a number of mutual funds do outperform their benchmark index.

So how does a broker decide what particular fund to recommend to Hyperactive Investors?

As with most other things within the financial services system, the recommendation decision is often driven by money.

Brokerage firms and brokers, and some independent advisors, are also paid a commission by the fund distributor when they sell a particular mutual fund.

Brokerage firms in the United States are paid for "shelf space" so they will recommend some mutual funds and not others. Charles Schwab, the founder of one of the largest discount brokerage firms, used the metaphor of the financial supermarket to try to get investors to understand that they could come to Schwab and buy any mutual fund, from any "brand" or fund family. And, just like supermarkets, Schwab and other brokerage firms started charging mutual fund managers for preferential treatment.

This preferential treatment goes both ways—sometimes brokerage firms that sell enough mutual fund shares to their retail customers are also given favourable treatment by the mutual fund manager, who trades shares in the stocks that are bought and sold for the mutual fund through the brokerage firm's institutional brokerage arm.

In Canada, the mutual fund company pays a commission— of usually about 5%—to the dealer who sold you its fund. This charge accrues to investors who buy mutual funds with a deferred sales charge and sell them within a set period of time. A portion of this commission goes to the advisor who recommended the fund to you.

In addition, the fund company pays ongoing commissions to advisors and dealers "for ongoing service and advice." These commissions are called *trailer fees* and vary in amount from 1% on front-load accounts to 0.5% on deferred sales accounts. Your advisor usually receives a portion of these fees as well.

Canadian investors who buy mutual funds directly from financial institutions and mutual fund companies that deal directly with the public can avoid these charges by purchasing "no-load" mutual funds.

If you read the fine print of any mutual fund **prospectus**, these fees are disclosed. But you really have to be a diligent reader.

> A **PROSPECTUS** is a document that should be given to a potential investor before he or she makes an investment. Every mutual fund has a prospectus, as does an initial public offering of stock. The prospectus defines the risks of the potential investment, as well as the investment philosophy and the capitalization of the stock or mutual fund the investor is being solicited to invest in.

I have never met an investor who realized that the brokerage firm he or she deals with regularly receives a financial inducement to make mutual fund recommendations.

It is bad enough that there is no evidence to support a hyperactive broker's claims about his or her ability to select mutual funds that will beat the market. Indeed, there is compelling evidence to the contrary: mutual funds sold by brokers and advisors have historically *underperformed* those purchased directly by investors. But it is worse that his or her recommendations are influenced by payments from mutual fund companies.

If you need another reason not to use hyperactive brokers or advisors, this is a good one. Smart Investors do not require the advice of brokers or advisors. But, if they do decide to go this route, they use those whose advice is totally objective, and not influenced by fees received on the basis of the funds they recommend.

Chapter 18

Hyperactive Investing Is Expensive

Investing is a strange business. It's the only one we know of where the more expensive the products get, the more customers want to buy them.
—Anthony M. Gallea and William Patalon III,
Contrarian Investing

Why pay more to achieve less? The costs imposed on the clueless Hyperactive Investors are one of the major reasons why they fare so poorly.

This is particularly the case in Canada, where fees charged by actively managed funds are significantly higher than comparable fees in the United States.

The stated "management expense ratio" of the average hyperactive Canadian mutual fund (i.e., the cost of running the fund—a cost borne by the fund's investors) is 2.4% of the fund's total assets. This is the cost of salaries and other compensation (which is often high), utilities, computers and telecommunications, research services and explicit marketing costs such as glossy brochures, and lunch for retail brokers when the mutual fund "wholesaler" goes to visit and pitch his or her wares.

In addition, Canadian investors may also pay a front-end load charge of 4% or more of their total investment (the amount is negotiable), which they could avoid by buying a no-load fund typically sold by banks or directly by certain fund families.

Although the mutual fund industry in Canada has grown exponentially, the savings resulting from economies of scale have not been passed on to Canadian mutual fund investors. Indeed, the management expense ratios of Canadian mutual funds have actually increased during this period of growth.

Think about that for a moment. If, in a given year, the relevant benchmark for one of these funds returns 10%, to achieve the goal of beating the market, a front-end-loaded hyperactive fund with an expense ratio of 2.4% and a front-end load of 4% would have to return more than 16.4%. And these costs do not include taxes, which are paid by the investor, depending on his or her tax circumstances, and can significantly reduce the investor's net return on the average mutual fund investment.

The average cost of ETFs that seek market returns is typically less than 0.30%. Since most Smart Investors do not need the advice of any advisor, their expenses can generally be kept to about 0.30%, plus the transaction cost of purchasing the ETFs, a savings of about 2% on investments in hyperactively managed funds. On a $100,000 investment, that is $2000 in the first year! In a slowly rising market, the amount saved will gradually increase from $2000 in each successive year. This is money in the Smart Investor's pocket rather than on the mutual fund company's profit line or in the coffers of the hyperactive brokerage firm.

And the taxes paid on ETFs are a fraction of those incurred by hyperactive funds. This is because limited trading is performed by ETFs. They only buy or sell shares in a stock when that company comes into or falls out of the particular index they are matching.

The difference between the internal costs of hyperactive funds and those invested for market returns is a primary reason why you should become a Smart Investor. ETFs have such a significant cost advantage that they are likely to outperform hyperactive funds by approximately the difference in these fund management costs.

In this case, you don't get what you pay for. The *less* expensive product is the superior one.

I know this is counterintuitive, but when you understand the relationship between low transaction costs, lower taxes (due to significantly less trading) and superior performance, you are well on your way to understanding why you have a responsibility, for your sake and for the financial security of your loved ones, to become a Smart Investor.

Have I convinced you yet? If so, you can skip right to Chapter 33, which describes the four-step process for achieving vastly superior market returns.

Chapter 19

If It Walks like a Duck and Quacks like a Duck...

[T]here's not a single good reason to invest in a bank wrap. The fees are comparatively high, the returns all too often are mediocre or worse and the methodology behind them can be questionable.
—Rob Carrick, "Bank-Sold Wrap Accounts Don't Live Up to Sales Pitch," *Globe and Mail,* April 4, 2004. Reported at: https://secure.globeadvisor.com/servlet/ArticleNews/story/gam/20041204/STMAIN04

It probably is a duck.

Financial advisors at banks and brokers have become very successful in convincing Canadian Hyperactive Investors to pay an annual management fee—a so-called wrap fee—instead of a commission on fund or stock purchases. These firms frequently charge fees ranging from 1.5% to 3% of the portfolio's value as a wrap fee.

A wrap account is a managed account, usually managed by selected outside fund managers. Investors are told this is a good deal because they are not being charged commissions and they get access to fund managers otherwise available only to very large investors. A much-touted added benefit is the fact that wrap accounts offer pre-packaged blends of mutual funds, thereby offering investors "one-stop shopping" with built-in asset allocation.

The sales blitz for wrap accounts has been very successful. As of December 31, 2004, Canadian investors had sunk $84 billion into these accounts. That number is projected to increase to more than $195 billion by 2012.

Investors aren't told that these fund managers have no more ability to pick stocks or to time the markets than a "financial astrologer" or a hyperactive broker or advisor acting on his or her own.

In reality, wrap accounts are a way for advisors to generate significant fees for doing very little work. The advisory firm typically pays 1% of the investor's assets to the manager(s), and gets to keep 1% or 1.5% (or more) of the investor's assets, split between the firm and the individual broker. The investor essentially pays 1.5% to 3% of his or her assets for the privilege of investing with fund managers who have no better chance of beating market returns than mutual fund managers who charge a lower fee—and you have seen how unlikely it is that even *these* managers can beat the markets.

It really doesn't matter if you invest in a mutual fund or a wrap account. If either or both are hyperactively managed, they are poor choices.

The bottom line is that the combination of higher costs, lower performance and greater tax consequences make all investments touted as being able to beat the markets worse than a zero-sum game, which is why Smart Investors avoid them.

Chapter 20

Brokers Understand Fees but Not Risk

Odds are you don't know what the odds are.
—Gary Belsky and Thomas Gilovich, *Why Smart People Make Big Money Mistakes*

Costs incurred are one of the two major differences between Smart Investors and Hyperactive Investors. The other difference is that Smart Investors understand risk and Hyperactive Investors do not.

There is a way to mathematically measure how risky an investment or a portfolio really is. Called **standard deviation**, this method has been accepted as the most appropriate way to measure the risk in investment portfolios since the work of Harry Markowitz in the late 1950s. Markowitz won the Nobel Prize in Economics for his research—research those hyperactive brokers and advisors either ignore or don't know about.

> **STANDARD DEVIATION** measures the volatility of a security or of a portfolio of securities. Specifically, it measures the fluctuation of stock prices without regard to direction. Standard deviation is measured using a statistical calculation. It is important for every investor to know, and to understand the significance of, the standard deviation of his or her investment portfolio.

I look at standard deviation in investing the same way I look at the results of my blood tests. I don't really need to understand how the lab arrived at the numbers, but I do need to know what is within normal range.

In investing, the higher the standard deviation, the more risky the portfolio. Here are some general guidelines, using the fall 2005 standard deviation of the S&P/TSX Composite Index as a guide:

- Conservative investors should have a standard deviation no higher than 8%.
- Moderately aggressive investors should have a standard deviation no higher than 15%.
- Very aggressive investors should have a standard deviation no higher than 20%.
- No one should have a standard deviation higher than 30%, if that.

For most investors, that is all you need to know about standard deviation. And that is more than most hyperactive brokers and advisors know.

Go ahead—ask your advisor what the standard deviation of your portfolio is. If he or she can compute it for you, right there in the office, without asking for help, I will be stunned. In any event, if the percentage exceeds these guidelines, Smart Investors should get concerned.

Chapter 21

Too Many Stocks, Too Few Bonds

Investment policy [asset allocation] is the foundation upon which portfolios should be constructed and managed.
—Charles D. Ellis, *Investment Policy*

Another important factor in proper investing—after taking account of costs and understanding risk—is asset allocation. Asset allocation refers to the percentage of an investment portfolio held in each of the major asset classes—stocks, bonds and cash.

Many academic studies have shown that the vast majority of a portfolio's variability in returns is accounted for by asset allocation. Very little is accounted for by either market timing or by picking the "right" security within an asset class. Therefore, it is curious that all the hype you hear from hyperactive brokers and advisors relates to market timing and stock picking.

When is the last time your hyperactive broker called you for the sole purpose of discussing your asset allocation?

Most Hyperactive Investors have portfolios that are under-weighted in bonds and overweighted in stocks. They are invested in this manner because their advisors have told them that stocks will outperform bonds in the long term. Younger investors are told that they should hold a higher percentage of stocks in their portfolios because they have more time to deal with the bad years and, over time, stocks will outperform bonds.

This is basically true. The average annualized return of the S&P/TSX Composite Index since 1957 was 10.57%. During this same time period, the average annualized return of long-term government bonds was 8.20%. These averages are before taking into account inflation and taxes.

However, although stocks have historically outperformed bonds, there are long periods of time where this has not been the case. For example, for the period from January 1990 through December 2002, Canadian bonds averaged 9.7% and Canadian equities averaged only 7.2%.

In addition, there is compelling evidence that investment risk does not always decline over time. Therefore, it is by no means always true that younger investors should hold most of their portfolio in stocks.

Bonds are an important part of your portfolio for reasons other than their performance relative to stocks. The performance of bonds does not correlate highly with the performance of stocks. This means that bond prices do not move in tandem with stock prices.

This is perfectly logical. The psychology of investing—often at the urging of hyperactive brokers and advisors—leads people to move money out of bonds when the stock market is rising and into bonds when the stock market is sinking. When the price of one asset gets low enough, there will be buyers who perceive it as undervalued, and when the price gets high enough there will be sellers who perceive it as overvalued.

When you have two asset classes in your portfolio that do not correlate highly with each other, you minimize your risk significantly.

The clear import of this data is that bonds should be part of almost every portfolio, in varying percentages. (You'll learn how to determine the correct percentage for your portfolio in Chapter 34.)

Typically, hyperactive brokers and advisors ignore this truth. They do so because bonds are not as sexy as stocks. There is not as much opportunity for a steep rise in price. But it is because of this steadier, less volatile performance over time that bonds should be used as ballast in every portfolio, to keep it on an even keel.

Smart Investors understand that an appropriate allocation of bonds in their portfolios is critical to risk management.

Chapter 22

Risk and Reward

[I]f you can form a portfolio that performs exactly average—i.e., identically to the whole market—you will outperform most actively trading investors.
—Jeremy Siegel, Ph.D., Russell E. Palmer Professor of Finance, The Wharton School. "Indexing Your Portfolio: The Evolution of Indices," *The Future for Investors,* July 3, 2006. Reported at: http://finance.yahoo.com/columnist/article/futureinvest/6953

Everyone wants to make as big a return as he or she can. But at what risk?

The possibility of gaining a few percentage points on the upside may be dwarfed by the increase in downside risk.

Take a look at the chart on page 74, which illustrates this point.

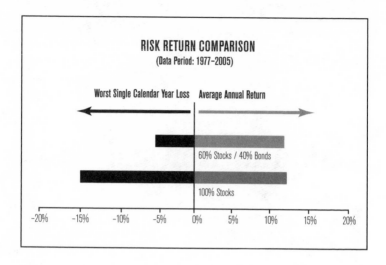

As you can see, if you invested in a diversified portfolio consisting of 100% stocks during the period 1977 to 2005, your average return would have been **11.7%**. Your worst loss in any one calendar year would have been **15.1%**.

However, if you had a diversified portfolio invested in only 60% stocks and 40% bonds, your average return would have been **11.0%**—only 0.7% less than the 100% stock portfolio. However, your worst loss in any one year—instead of being 15.1% with the 100% stock portfolio—would have been only **6.2%**.

By moving from a portfolio that is 100% invested in stocks to one that is 60% invested in stocks and 40% invested in government bonds, it is possible to greatly reduce the downside risk while sacrificing only a modest amount of upside potential.

Is it worth it to you to squeeze an extra 0.7% on the upside, if that means accepting the possibility of losing an additional 9% on the downside? The answer to this question will depend on a number of factors, including the investment objectives, age and tolerance for risk of each investor.

Now, there is a classic objection put forward by those who are invested 100% in stocks or those who suggest that their clients invest 100% in stocks. That argument has to do with the long term versus the short term. It is true that, over the long term, stocks have a better return than bonds. Therefore, they argue, anyone investing for the long term should be better off investing completely in stocks.

There are, however, two problems with this argument.

The first has to do with timing. You never know when stocks will have a run of one, two, three or even more consecutive down years. If those happen to be the years an investor needs to cash out of a major portion of his or her investments, or if the investor simply does not have the stomach to tolerate those losses, then the investor may be forced to sell at the worst possible time.

The second has to do with the basic fallacy of hyperactive investing. Hyperactive brokers and advisors often tell their clients to sell stocks or mutual funds that are on the way down and to invest in stocks or funds that are on the way up. But in a market that is generally moving down, even the stocks or funds that are moving up may not move up enough to counter the losses in the previous investments, or may not move up for very long.

I will say that some Smart Investors—those who are investing in funds that match the broadest stock market indexes and who can commit *without reservation* to holding those funds for the long term—can safely hold a fairly large percentage of their portfolio in stocks. But I still don't believe anyone should be invested 100% in stocks.

Hyperactive brokers and advisors typically do not present data in this manner. Nor do they ask these kinds of questions. Their focus is exclusively on the upside. Timing the market, picking stocks and finding hot fund managers all speak to the upside. Marketing is all about the upside.

Smart Investors never lose sight of the downside risks.

Chapter 23

Beware of House Funds!

If [expense ratios] are higher on in-house funds, insist on proof the pick is meant to improve your net worth rather than the firm's.
— Jonathan Chevreau, "Another Way to Lose Your Money," *National Post,* January 11, 2003

House funds are hyperactively managed funds created, owned and managed by brokerage firms. They can be sold only by brokers who work for that firm. They usually bear the name of the brokerage firm that sponsors them (for example, the Altamira Capital Growth Fund).

There is no evidence that house funds are a good investment.

One study compared the performance of the house funds of American Express, Smith Barney, Prudential, Merrill Lynch and Morgan Stanley for a 10-year period with similar funds managed by well-known independent fund families.

The house funds got trounced.

Brokers typically earn a larger commission for selling these funds. It is not surprising that they recommend them to their clients.

There is no reason to buy a house fund.

This dismal performance record raises a much bigger issue: If the big brokerage firms cannot manage their own funds more successfully, why should you rely on them for advice?

The answer is that you shouldn't, and, for that matter, you shouldn't buy any hyperactively managed fund.

Advisors to Smart Investors do not work for companies that own, manage or operate their own hyperactive funds. Because they don't work for companies with proprietary funds, they have no perverse incentive to recommend funds that, when objectively viewed, underperform.

Smart Investors never buy house funds, or any hyperactively managed funds. Neither should you.

Chapter 24

Beware of Margin!

There's little worse for an investor than the experience of taking out a loan to purchase stocks, mutual funds or investment property, and then watching as the value of the leveraged portfolio declines, leaving the investor on the hook for the loan interest.

—David Cruise and Alison Griffiths, "It's Unwise to Chase Yesterday's Winners," *Toronto Star*, July 2, 2006. Reported at: http://www.thestar.com/NASApp/cs/ContentServer?pagename =thestar/Layout/Article_Type1&c=Article&cid=1151791810 427&call_pageid=968350072197&col=969048863851

Warning: *Margin May Be Disastrous to Your Financial Health.*

When using "margin," an investor puts up the shares he or she owns as collateral against a cash loan that permits the purchase of additional securities.

Margin increases risk.

Since most hyperactive brokers and advisors don't know how to measure risk, investors who buy on margin are rarely aware of the effect margin has on risk. Margin magnifies risk—dramatically—by allowing an investor to purchase more of a security than he or she has cash to back up the purchase.

If the value of the security drops, the ratio of collateral to loan is reduced, and the investor must either come up with more cash or sell some of the security in order to reduce the amount of the loan and bring the ratio back into balance.

Of course, margin is great for the brokerage firm, which charges interest on the margin loan. This may or may not be shared with the broker in the form of a bonus or some sort of "soft money" credit, such as an increase in the amount the broker can charge to the firm for individual marketing expenses. For the firm, there is no risk in margin. It is a pure profit centre.

Smart Investors never buy on margin. They have no reason to do so.

Chapter 25

Beware of Hedge Funds!

It's amateur hour in the hedge fund business. This sideshow of sometimes bizarre (and always costly) investing is on a tear like never before. It's attracting some of the shrewdest and sharpest minds on Wall Street—and also shills, shysters, charlatans and neophytes too crooked or too stupid to make any money for you.
— Neil Weinberg and Bernard Condon, "The Sleaziest Show on Earth," *Forbes,* May 24, 2004. Reported at: http://www.forbes.com/global/2004/0524/030_print.html

The "hot" investment of the twenty-first century is the hedge fund, many of which specialize in making large investments in a few positions, which sets up the possibility for either outsized returns or outsized losses. Others use a so-called market neutral strategy, which hedges these big bets with counterweight investments (hence the term *hedge fund*).

Canadian investors have sunk more than $30 billion into these funds. Most of these investors have no idea how risky these funds are and precious little data is available to assist them. Unfortunately, there is no end of marketing hype encouraging Canadians to invest in hedge funds. Much of this hype is extremely misleading and includes statements about how hedge funds will make money "in any market" and why they are really less volatile than mutual funds.

Hedge funds in Canada are very loosely regulated. In general, "accredited investors" must have assets (net of liabilities) in excess of $1,000,000 or net pre-tax income greater than $200,000. However, the securities industry in Canada has found some loopholes in the regulatory scheme so that otherwise non-accredited investors are able to hop on the hedge fund freight train.

Much of the activity is generated by hyperactive brokers and advisors, who sometimes recommend investments in hedge funds to clients for whom such an investment is completely inappropriate.

This frenzy is driven by—you guessed it—fees.

Hedge funds typically charge 20% of profits plus 1% to 2% of assets managed. This is a previously unheard-of fee structure. Brokers and advisors receive significant fees for recommending hedge funds to their clients.

All you need to know about why you should not invest in hedge funds is outlined in the *Forbes* magazine article cited at the beginning of this chapter.

For starters:

- The performance of these funds is often overstated. (For example, 26,000 investors—mostly Canadians—are likely to lose a significant portion of the $800 million invested in Portus Alternative Asset Management. The hedge fund declared bankruptcy in March 2006, and its co-founder fled the country after the Ontario Securities Commission began an investigation of the fund).

- Hedge funds are illiquid; you generally must leave your full investment in the fund for a predetermined period of time before it can be redeemed.
- You hear about the winners, but not about the losers.
- The cozy relationship between some funds and some major brokerage firms is troublesome.
- Hedge funds have an extremely short lifespan, averaging less than 3.5 years, thereby depriving investors of the ability to analyze long-term returns.
- There is no way investors can predict which of the 110 or so hedge funds available to Canadian investors might outperform a broad market index in the future. This uncertainty is best illustrated by a study I undertook. I looked at the 110 hedge funds in Canada that had a three-year record of returns, for the period ending May 31, 2006. Only 14 of them (12.73%) outperformed the S&P/TSX Composite Index.

Most investors should not invest in a hedge fund. For those who do, the investment should be limited to a very small percentage of their portfolio.

Hyperactive brokers and advisors love hedge funds. The commissions are great.

Chapter 26

Value Stocks—Reward Without Risk?

Most people want candy, when what they really need is a balanced meal.

—John J. Bowen, Jr., *The Prudent Investor's Guide to Beating Wall Street at Its Own Game*

The term **value stocks** refers to stocks that trade at a low price relative to their "fundamentals." Fundamentals can mean factors like dividends, earnings or sales. Many advisors and authors of financial books—hyped by the financial media—believe that investing in these companies is a way to beat the market.

Is this the magic bullet?

The short answer is a resounding "no!"

Supporters of buying value stocks cite data showing that value stocks, and particularly small value stocks, historically outperform other sectors.

For example, for the 78-year period from 1927 to 2004, an index of U.S. small value stocks had annual average returns of 14.6% per year. For the same time period, an index of U.S. large growth stocks had annual average returns of only 9.5%.

So, why not have a portfolio of all small value stocks?

Because of the risk—or uncertainty of returns—of such a portfolio.

Remember our discussion of the use of standard deviation to measure risk in Chapter 20? We can measure risk with mathematical precision.

The standard deviation of a portfolio consisting only of an index of small value stocks during this time period would have been a whopping 34.9%. What does this mean in practical terms?

It means that this is an extremely volatile portfolio not suitable for *anyone*. The rare exception might be a very young person, with the ability to replace significant losses with ease. As you will recall, I told you that the most aggressive investor should not have a portfolio that exceeds a standard deviation of 30%, and this portfolio (at more than 30%) is off the charts!

How volatile is this portfolio? Well, based on its standard deviation and historical returns, it is likely that, 68% of the time, the value of this portfolio can be expected to have returns ranging from an annual gain of 49.5% to an annual *loss* of as much as 20.3%. Is that enough to keep you awake at night?

Let's compare this kind of volatility with the high-risk portfolio in the chart in Chapter 4. This is the most aggressive of the four portfolios I recommend for Smart Investors.

Sixty-eight percent of the time, the value of this portfolio can be expected to have returns ranging from an annual gain of 25% to an annual loss of as much as 1%.

Quite a difference from a portfolio consisting of all small value stocks.

The four portfolios I recommend give Smart Investors the benefit of the historical higher returns of value stocks, without the unacceptable volatility caused by over-concentration of your portfolio in this sector.

Every stock in the market is either value or growth, or some combination of value and growth. **Growth stocks** are typically thought of as stocks in companies that have rapidly growing sales, revenues and profits, and that plow most of those returns back into growing the company rather than paying a dividend to shareholders.

Many investors divide the world of stocks into **GROWTH STOCKS** and **VALUE STOCKS**. While growth stocks are stocks of rapidly growing companies, value stocks are stocks in companies whose perceived value as assigned by the market is below the value assigned by the particular analyst. The notion of value is truly in the eye of the beholder. Some successful investors, such as Warren Buffett, have made a career of being "value investors"— finding "undervalued" investments and taking large stakes in them.

The market is defined as being equally divided between growth and value. Therefore, when you hold the ETFs I recommend in this book, you are holding half of your stock portfolio in growth and half in value.

No reputable advisor would recommend a portfolio of all small value stocks for anyone, except in the most unusual circumstances. It is just too volatile and risky.

And it gets worse. If you follow the advice of some financial gurus and use their special criteria for selecting a limited number of these stocks, instead of buying an ETF consisting of the thousands of stocks that are available in this sector, your standard deviation will increase, making your portfolio even more volatile.

Here is the bottom line: Investing all of your assets in any one sector of the market—especially a volatile sector—is foolhardy. It appeals to greed, but it is equivalent to rank speculation. The risk of significant losses is enormously increased. The risk of greatly enhanced volatility is all but assured.

Don't do it.

Chapter 27

Why Hasn't Anyone Told You?

My research [of Canadian equity mutual funds] (and virtually all studies looking at funds in other countries) indicates that mutual fund managers on average underperform their risk-adjusted benchmarks.
—Richard Deaves, Ph.D., professor of finance, DeGroote School of Business, McMaster University, *What Kind of an Investor Are You?*

You have to give great credit to hyperactive brokers and advisors. They have told a story that feeds into human psychology at a host of different levels. They have successfully marketed skills they don't have. They are able to keep Hyperactive Investors so confused and disoriented that these poor folks don't realize there is a much better alternative. And, by doing so, they have made a whole lot of money.

By all accounts, the average compensation of Canadian financial advisors is upwards of $100,000 per year, even in difficult years for the markets as a whole. And top-earning advisors are paid as much as $570,000. This puts many advisors in the top echelons of all Canadian earners. Not bad for someone who ignores basic principles of finance and is selling a hope and a dream, with precious little to back them up.

Conversely, advisors to Smart Investors have typically marketed well to large investors—endowments, pension plans and trusts—but poorly to the individual-investor market.

To be sure, there is enough money available from large investors for an entire cadre of these advisors to collectively earn a nice living. And it is much easier to explain the concept of Smart Investing to people who understand basic financial concepts, which many individual investors do not.

But those of us who advise our clients to become Smart Investors have been abdicating our responsibility to advise the millions of Hyperactive Investors. Perhaps it is because we have no financial incentive to provide this advice since, as I have said, most Smart Investors do not need our services to reach their financial goals.

The Vanguard Group, and especially the company's founder, John Bogle, is a notable exception to this rule. It was Bogle and Vanguard that created the opportunity for all investors to invest for market returns, by establishing index funds with low initial investments (as little as US$2500), low annual expenses and a coherent set of marketing materials. Unfortunately, regulations enacted by the Ontario Securities Commission and provincial securities regulators make it difficult, if not impossible, for Canadian investors to purchase these funds or, for that matter, to access other lower cost index funds available to U.S. residents. Fortunately, however, a number of low-cost index funds and ETFs are now available to Canadian investors.

While a number of books have been written about the virtues of being a Smart Investor, few have achieved commercial success. One exception is *A Random Walk Down Wall Street,* a superb book by Burton Malkiel, now in its eighth edition.

Malkiel, a professor of economics at Princeton University, was one of the first to show that the history of the price of a stock cannot be used to predict how it will move in the future, and therefore that stock price movement is, in the language of economists, "random." In other words, he completely debunked the belief that anyone can consistently predict the future prices of stocks (which is the core belief of Hyperactive Investors!).

Most of the books and articles written on the merits of being a Smart Investor are, unfortunately, dense and difficult to understand—thus seemingly validating the myth that being a Smart Investor is somehow elitist, complex and beyond the ability of the ordinary investor.

Nothing could be farther from the truth.

Chapter 28

The Financial Media Are Part of the Problem

But there is no one around to hold the financial media accountable for its actions when it steers investors into making poor decisions with their money. When "The Best Five Stocks" turn out to be a poor investment, does anybody care about the retired couple that followed that advice and had their retirement funds depleted? Apparently not.

—Daniel M. Wheeler, director of global financial advisor services, Dimensional Fund Advisors. "Tools of the Trade: Don't Believe the Hype," *Investment Advisor,* May 2005. Reprinted at: http://www.dfaus.com/library/reprints/ tools_hype

The financial media, in both Canada and the United States, are part of the problem. In fact, the large brokerage firms are major advertisers in the financial media. As a result, the financial media are very dependent upon these firms' goodwill. This means that the articles written in the financial media don't usually challenge the hyperactive broker or advisor's basic marketing thrust—trading.

Members of the brokerage community often are contributors to the "news" featured in the financial media. How many times have we all seen on television an interview with a brokerage firm analyst or "market strategist" where he or she is standing in front of the company's name? This is little more than free marketing. The person could be reciting a directory of Toronto phone listings and it wouldn't matter to his or her firm. Every second that company logo is there in the background amounts to thousands of dollars that doesn't have to be spent on advertising.

It is not surprising that this participation contributes to the popular image that hyperactive brokers and advisors actually add value and are worthy of deference from beleaguered investors. It is in the interest of the financial media to break news—daily, weekly or monthly—because they need to sell magazines or newspapers, or to achieve or maintain high viewer ratings. The financial media contribute to the false impression that investors must always be on top of the latest news, lest they miss an investment opportunity.

Some "investment" television shows are little more than tabloid journalism, and some self-styled investment gurus have resorted to behaviour that can only be described as maniacal. This may be entertaining to some, but it should not be confused with any recognized principles of finance that might assist investors in making intelligent decisions about managing their assets.

Even the more serious shows encourage false beliefs—beliefs that are harmful to investors. The financial media, like astrologers, convey the message that predicting the future is the key to successful investing.

As ludicrous as this may be, it sells papers and it sells advertising time. In order to make sure it sells, the media publishes and airs no end of predictions from "experts" who appear, in fact, to know the future. We all have seen the stories, ranging from "The One Stock Everyone Must Own" to "The Hottest Mutual Funds for Next Year."

But the advice these stories give is often erroneous and misleading. I give some examples of this erroneous advice in the next chapter, which is aptly entitled "Financial Pornography," because that is what this "advice" is.

Even if you find the financial media entertaining, you should ignore everything you read in the magazines and newspapers, everything you see and hear on the television and everything that you pay to have pumped into your Palm Pilot or BlackBerry that purports to tell you where the markets are headed or whether or not a particular stock or fund should be bought or sold.

The financial media (with rare exceptions, such as Canadian economic journalist Jonathan Chevreau, *The Wall Street Journal*'s Jonathan Clements, and well-respected American economic journalist Jane Bryant Quinn) are part of the problem. Everything about them—from the ads to the opinions to the news—is nothing more than hype masquerading as critical information that Hyperactive Investors must absorb in their quest to beat the markets.

If you become a Smart Investor, you won't need any of it.

Chapter 29

"Financial Pornography"

I was getting at the newspapers and magazines that make investing sound easy. "Three ways to double your money." "Ten hot stocks." The articles that make it sound like the journalist knows the right stocks or mutual funds to buy. And the fact is, we don't know. Journalists don't have any business pretending they're investment analysts. We can talk about stocks, investment ideas and what people are saying. But journalists shouldn't say that certain stocks will increase in value. Nobody knows. Soft-core, though— the Net is hard-core.

—Jane Bryant Quinn. Interview with ABC News, August 1998

"Financial pornography" refers to the endless predictions made in the financial media. The term is generally credited to Jane Bryant Quinn, who writes about economic issues in a syndicated column.

These predictions are intended to sell books, magazines and newspapers, or to garner viewers and thus sell television advertising time.

But financial pornography also serves to convince investors that they can beat the markets if they buy the right books, magazines and newspapers, and watch the right television shows.

The predictions of these publications and shows are often terribly wrong and misguided, but they have served their intended purpose: Hyperactive Investors continue to believe that the answer is "out there" somewhere. They just have to keep studying hard enough and pay attention to the financial media and to the hyperactive brokers and advisors who provide the predictions in the financial media.

In a 1999 article, "Confessions of a Former Mutual Funds Reporter," a former *Fortune* magazine journalist, who understandably wishes to remain anonymous, stated, "we were preaching buy-and-hold marriage while implicitly endorsing hot-fund promiscuity." Why did *Fortune* do this? Because "unfortunately, rational, pro-index-fund stories don't sell magazines, cause hits on websites or boost Nielsen ratings."

Here are some examples of financial pornography.

The July 1993 cover of *Forbes* featured an amusing picture of Barton Biggs, who was then the chief global strategist of Morgan Stanley. Biggs donned a bear costume for the occasion. The article featured Biggs' advice to sell U.S. stocks and buy the stocks of emerging-economy growth markets.

Following his advice would have been an unmitigated disaster. Emerging-market stocks plunged for the next three years.

In November 2000, the venerable *Fortune* magazine set forth the "top picks" of its panelists of "top" stock analysts.

Between November 2000 and November 2003, here is how those predictions fared:

S&P 500	−22%
NASDAQ	−41%
Fortune Picks	−80%

In August 1979, *Business Week* magazine featured a story entitled "The Death of Equities." The story, true to its name, opined that "the death of equities is a near-permanent condition."

Almost immediately after the story's publication, far from "dying," stocks began one of the great bull markets in history.

And who can forget all of the bullish advice during the tech boom to focus on the tech sector and ignore investment fundamentals? Investors who followed the predictions and advice of these "investment gurus" lost up to 80% of their portfolios' value when the tech bubble exploded.

Sometimes the financial media are right. Sometimes they are wrong. When they are right, it is luck and not skill.

Hyperactive Investors rely on the financial media first to suggest to them what they should do, then to validate what they have done. Why would you rely on a source of information that is so frequently wrong and misleading, and that has a vested economic interest in keeping its ratings up so that it can increase its advertising revenues?

More important, why would you go back to the hyperactive brokers and advisors who are featured in much of the financial media and rely on them for financial advice when the predictions they make so publicly are often without any basis in fact?

Smart Investors pay no attention to the predictions made in the financial media, and never use them as a basis for their investment decisions.

If you become a Smart Investor, you can still read the financial media—but only for its entertainment value.

Chapter 30

Should Your Broker Act Only in Your Best Interest and Be Careful with Your Money?

[T]he relationship of broker and client is not, in and of itself, a fiduciary relationship but one that is dependent on the particular facts.
—Chesebrough v. Willson, decision of the Court of Appeal for Ontario, November 12, 2002

Most investors repose great trust and confidence in their brokers and investment advisors, relying on the advice these professionals provide. Investors often believe that these advisors have the highest possible duty of loyalty to them, much like a solicitor has to a client.

Unfortunately, this is not always the case. Whether or not a broker or advisor will be held to this high standard (known as a "fiduciary relationship") depends on the details of the actual relationship between the broker and the client.

I can think of no reason why *any* investor who is relying to *any* extent on advice given by his or her broker or advisor would do business with anyone who would not agree *in writing* to be held to the highest standard of loyalty and not to some lesser standard. At the very least, every client of a broker or investment advisor who holds this expectation should request a written confirmation that his or her broker or advisor accepts the role of a fiduciary in connection with all advice given to him or her.

Assuming that this hurdle can be overcome, do you believe that your broker or advisor should at least be required to be careful with your hard-earned money?

The Prudent Investor Rule governs the conduct of trustees of pension plans, trusts and similar funds in most states in the United States. Trillions of dollars of assets are managed by these trustees.

After all, being "prudent" is a pretty low standard. It only requires your hyperactive broker to be careful when he or she invests your money.

The Reporter's Notes to the 1994 *Uniform Prudent Investor Act* (often referred to as the Prudent Man Rule) sets forth the following:

[F]iduciaries and other investors are confronted with potent evidence that the application of expertise, investigation and diligence in efforts to beat the market in these publicly traded securities ordinarily promises little or no payoff or even a negative payoff after taking account of research and transaction costs.

Translation: Investors should seek market returns and not engage in stock picking or market timing in an effort (usually fruitless) to beat the markets.

While the standards for trustees in Canada vary by province, they also require a high standard of care. For example, Nova Scotia's *Trustee Act* provides that trustees must "exercise the care, skill, diligence and judgment that a prudent investor would exercise in making investments."

With these basic standards in mind, try this nugget out on the next broker or investment advisor who recommends the purchase of a "hot" stock or a "hot" mutual fund: "Do you follow the standard of care applicable to trustees in Nova Scotia (or in other provinces with similar requirements governing the conduct of trustees) in connection with the management of my account?" If the answer is "no," find out precisely what standard of care your broker is using and ask yourself whether you are comfortable with this standard. In my experience, most investors have no idea what standard of care is used by their brokers or investment advisors.

Personally, I would accept no lower standard of care than the one applied to the conduct of trustees.

Hyperactive brokers and advisors frequently fall short of this standard of care and ignore the "potent evidence" that active management is a loser's game.

Their daily grind consists of convincing you that they can beat the market because of their superior research and analytical abilities.

Check out the quotation from the Reporter's Notes to the *Uniform Prudent Investor Act* again. It says that this activity "ordinarily promises little or no payoff or even a negative payoff...."

If, when you opened an account with a hyperactive broker or advisor, that person candidly told you that he or she would be trying to beat the market but in all likelihood would not be able to and was actually likely to underperform the market, would you still do business with that person? Of course you would not. And you shouldn't.

Advisors to Smart Investors follow the letter and the spirit of the Prudent Investor Rule. They make no effort to time the market or to pick winners. They understand this "potent evidence."

You should follow their lead and do the same thing with your money.

PART THREE

Smart Investors Know Better

Chapter 31

Who Believes Me?

*In almost two decades on Wall Street, I have yet to see any
real evidence of successful market timing.*
—David M. Blitzer, Ph.D., managing director and chief
investment strategist and director of quantitative services,
Standard & Poor's, *Outpacing the Pros*

Currently in the United States, $550 billion is invested by
individuals in index stock mutual funds. But over $4 *trillion* is
invested in U.S. and international stock and bond indexes,
when these mutual fund investments are combined with the
investments of institutions such as pension funds, universities
and foundations. What do the managers of these institutions'
investment portfolios know that you don't? After all, they
could hire any hyperactive broker or advisor in the world, but
they elect not to do so.

Here is a very abbreviated list of U.S. institutional investors
with large Smart Investment portfolios:

Pension Funds (Each one has invested over $50 billion for
market returns.)
• California Public Employees Retirement System

- New York State Common
- California State Teachers
- New York State Teachers
- Florida State Board
- City of San Diego
- City of Seattle
- State of Maryland
- State of Utah
- Los Angeles City Employees Retirement Association

Educational Institutions
- California Institute of Technology
- Carnegie Mellon University
- Cornell University
- University of Miami

Religious and Charitable Organizations
- Catholic Superannuation Fund
- Jewish Community Foundation
- Salvation Army

A number of professional money management companies that manage large pools on behalf of institutions as well as wealthy individuals also utilize Smart Investing. Among them are

- Barclays Global Investors—managers of iShares, which are indexed to various benchmarks. Barclays manages over US$700 billion in indexed assets;
- State Street Global Advisors—manages over US$400 billion in indexed assets;

- Deutsche Asset Management—manages over US$145 billion in indexed assets; and
- TIAA-CREF—manages over US$100 billion in indexed assets.

To me, what is more telling even than these statistics is the list of individuals who either are Smart Investors or believe that individual investors should be Smart Investors. Many of them are quoted at the beginning of chapters in this book. Here are a few:

Nobel Laureates in Economics
- Daniel Kahneman
- Merton Miller
- Myron S. Scholes, who designed one of the most sophisticated pricing models for valuing stock options
- Paul A. Samuelson, author of one of the most widely used texts in general economics
- Robert C. Merton
- William F. Sharpe

Professors of Finance or Economics
- Burton G. Malkiel, professor of economics, Princeton University
- Eugene F. Fama, professor of finance, University of Chicago, and consultant to Dimensional Fund Advisors
- Rajeeva Sinha, professor of finance, Odette School of Business, University of Windsor
- Richard Deaves, professor of finance, DeGroote School of Business, McMaster University

- Roger G. Ibbotson, professor of finance, Yale University School of Management
- Vijay M. Jog, professor of finance, Eric Sprott School of Business, Carleton University

These professors have all done their work on the theoretical end of investing. But David F. Swensen, the chief investment officer of Yale University, who also teaches economics at Yale College and finance classes at Yale's School of Management, has lived investing from the trenches. He is the author of *Unconventional Success* (2005).

Swensen has made his professional name by running Yale's endowment fund, which has had superior growth through years when the market was up and when it was down. He has been involved in expanding the scope of the kind of investing done by university and other endowments, from venture capital investing to investing for social return within the local community, even to short-selling the market when he thought it was appropriate. Yet in his book Swensen says that for the vast majority of investors, Smart Investing is the way to go.

Two other men famous for their investing prowess, and who counsel investors to invest for market returns, are Peter Lynch and Warren Buffett.

Peter Lynch, the long-time manager of Fidelity's Magellan Fund in the 1980s and early 1990s, and probably the first of the "rock star" managers, is a fan of Smart Investing. This despite the fact that he is one of the icons of active managers, a person whom brokers and advisors continue to use to discredit the argument that no active manager can beat the market consistently. Lynch did it year in and year out for about a decade and went out a winner, retiring from active management for Fidelity to pursue other opportunities. As indexes have become more fine-tuned over time, and as the flow of information about investments has become more widespread over time, Lynch feels that the opportunities to find market inefficiencies have been essentially wiped out. The market *is* the return.

Warren Buffett, the "Sage of Omaha" and still chairperson of the Berkshire Hathaway company, is another legendary stock picker. Buffett's investments in industries and individual companies have, for years, had the power to move markets. But again, Buffett believes that efficient information flow and more indexing opportunities lead to greater market efficiency. Essentially, he says, market indexing will, over time, drive more market indexing.

This theory was recently validated in a study demonstrating that stock picking in the United States has declined from a high of 60% of the maximum fraction of the volume in the 1960s to a low of 24% in the 2000s, and there is compelling evidence that it will continue to decline. The authors of the study were so impressed with these findings that they concluded that "modern portfolio theory has won," meaning that markets are efficient and that stock picking is a fool's errand.

This conclusion is very significant, but it prompts the essential question: If Smart Investing accounts for the majority of the volume of trading in the United States, why do most individual investors continue to engage in the discredited practice of stock picking? And why do hyperactive brokers and advisors continue to advise them to do so?

The answer is very clear: Hyperactive brokers and advisors have no financial incentive to advise their clients to become Smart Investors. Together with the financial media, they are complicit in keeping this data from the average, hard-working individual investor.

So, which investors have received the message and account for the majority of the trading volume that engages in Smart Investing? Smart Investors, such as those managing pensions, trusts and corporate money.

If these Smart Investors—the most sophisticated funds and asset managers in the world—invest trillions of dollars for market returns, shouldn't your hard-earned assets be invested in the same manner?

The next time your hyperactive broker or advisor tells you about a "buying opportunity" in a stock or the next "hot" mutual fund, ask him to give you a written summary of his background and training in finance or economics. Compare it with the credentials of the aforementioned Nobel Prize winners, scholars, institutions and managers of megabillion-dollar university endowment funds.

Then reject his advice.

You want—and deserve—to be a Smart Investor.

Chapter 32

When Do Smart Investors Need an Advisor?

The expected return of the speculator is zero.
—Louis Bachelier, "The Theory of Speculation" (doctoral dissertation)

Most investors have under $1 million in assets available for investment. These investors can engage in Smart Investing by implementing one of the four portfolios I set forth in Chapter 36 **without relying on the advice of any broker or investment advisor**.

Larger investors, with more than $1 million in invested assets, pension plans and trusts, often can afford to pay an investment advisor. And some investment advisors can add value by adding a layer of complexity and fine tuning to the asset allocation strategies that I will talk about in the coming chapters.

This fine tuning for market returns usually adds some measure of extra benefit, without taking on extra risk. But it comes at a price: the management fee charged by an investment advisor.

Some of these advisors add real value by putting together relatively complex portfolios that seek a premium over market returns by using a fund family now available in Canada, called Dimensional Fund Advisors (DFA) (http://www.dfa canada.com/). (Full disclosure: I am a registered advisor in the United States and recommend DFA funds to my clients.) DFA manages more than US$100 billion for large institutional and individual investors. It does not engage in market timing or stock picking. All of its funds are passively managed, using a variant of index funds. DFA makes its funds available through selected fee-based investment advisors. You can find a list of these advisors on DFA's Canadian website.

If you decide to use an advisor, you should be wary of anyone who does not consider the lowest-cost options to implementing investment portfolios. The lowest-cost options typically are ETFs, low-cost index funds and the funds available to Canadian investors that are passively managed by DFA.

DFA and its network of economic and financial consultants, many of whom are university professors and some of whom are Nobel laureates, offer passive portfolios that are slightly different from ETFs and the typical index funds offered in Canada. (A comprehensive list of Canadian index funds can by found at http://globefunddb.theglobeand mail.com/gishome/plsql/gis.process_fr?fr_param1=index &fr_mode=FUNDNAME&iaction=Go.)

These differences are due to the way in which stocks are assigned to indexes. True index funds are rigid. They require that the portfolio match the components of the index exactly. The problem is that stocks that begin a year as part of a specific index may lose the characteristics that caused them to be assigned to the index.

For example, if a small stock has a run-up in price, it is no longer a small stock—it is a large stock. However, it will remain in small-stock indexes until the next time the index is reconstituted, which usually happens once a year. The stock will remain in small-stock index funds that are rigid in their composition. DFA would drop this stock from its passively managed small-stock fund when it ceased to be a small stock, instead of waiting for the index reconstitution.

DFA also offers funds that concentrate on more precisely defined sectors of the market than those in other fund families. Think of it like ice cream.

With typical index funds, you can have vanilla (a fund that holds all the stocks in the TSE 300, which is often used in financial shorthand as a proxy for the large-cap sector of the Canadian stock market).

You can have chocolate (a fund that invests in an index of Canadian mid-cap stocks).

You can have strawberry (a fund that invests in an index of Canadian **small-cap stocks**).

> The term **SMALL CAP** is a term used to describe companies with market values between US$300 million and US$2 billion.

Or you can have a couple of other flavours—funds that invest in other indexes.

DFA, on the other hand, has index funds that invest in the stocks of *all sorts* of very exotic "flavours," or market segments.

For instance, one limitation of many index fund families is that they don't offer index funds in the international small-cap and international value markets, whereas DFA does.

There is strong academic evidence that a portfolio tilted optimally towards value and small-cap equities will, over long holding periods, outperform the broader equity markets by as much as 1% to 2% per year. That can add up to a lot of money when it is compounded over many years. By "tilting" a portfolio towards these equities, I am referring to including a small percentage of these equities in your portfolio. This is not to be confused with the mistake of investing all of your assets in these asset classes (or in any one class), which I discussed in Chapter 26.

However, I do not believe that this "bang for the buck," particularly when you consider the added costs of advisors' fees, is worth it for investors with less than $1 million to invest. For these investors, the portfolios I recommend should more than satisfy their financial objectives. There are, however, well-respected finance professionals who would lower the threshold for using an advisor, and who can give investors access to DFA funds, for as little as $250,000.

Hyperactive brokers and advisors argue that it is small investors who need the extra "handholding" they can provide because investing is so complex, and the typical small investor cannot be expected to know how to conduct research into the best possible investments.

But, in truth, small investors don't need advice on how to make complex investments. What small investors need is actually very simple to implement: Everyone is always looking for something that correlates positively with superior portfolio performance. Every academic who has ever studied this problem has found two things that correlate with superior performance. One is low transaction costs. The other is appropriate asset allocation.

Investing with the goal of market returns and without incurring any advisory fees definitely meets the first test. I describe in the following chapters how investors can easily ensure that their portfolios are suitably allocated for their investment objectives and tolerance for risk. And for Smart Investors with less than $1 million to invest, this self-help strategy is the way to go.

PART FOUR

The Real Way Smart Investors Beat 95% of the "Pros"

Chapter 33

The Four-Step Process

Faced with the choice between changing one's mind and proving that there is no need to do so, almost everybody gets busy on the proof.
—John Kenneth Galbraith, late renowned Canadian-American economist

Being a Smart Investor is very simple. Just follow these four basic steps:

1. Decide on your asset allocation.
2. Open an account with an online Canadian broker, paying particular attention to the transaction fees charged by that broker for the purchase and sales of ETFs. Current rules of the Ontario Securities Commission prevent Canadian investors from doing business with U.S. brokers unless they are properly registered. Brokerage fees charged by U.S. brokers for ETF trades are generally lower than fees charged in Canada.
3. Invest the stock and bond portions of your portfolio in the ETFs described in this book.

4. Rebalance your portfolio twice a year to keep your portfolio either aligned with your original asset allocation or
   with a new asset allocation that meets your changed
   investment objectives and/or risk tolerance.

   That's it.
   Read on for more details on each step.

Chapter 34

Step 1: Determine Your Asset Allocation

Over 90% of investment returns are determined by how investors allocate their assets versus security selection, market timing and other factors.
—Brinson, Singer and Beebower, "Determinants of Portfolio Performance II: An Update," *Financial Analysts Journal,* May–June 1991

Asset allocation is the division of an investment portfolio among three types of investments—stocks, bonds and cash equivalents such as certificates of deposit. Asset allocation is the big decision you need to make. All the other decisions are small.

Stocks historically have provided the highest returns and the greatest risks.

Bonds provide significantly lower returns than stocks but at lower risk.

Cash, the term for short-term, highly liquid investments, barely keeps up with inflation, but is very close to risk-free.

By splitting your portfolio up among these asset classes, you can target the specific level of return you wish to get for the specific level of risk you are willing to take. Economists have very accurately modelled how different balances among these three asset classes affect both return and risk within a portfolio.

Academic research has shown that asset allocation accounts for 90% or more of the variability of returns from any particular portfolio. The specific securities held in the portfolio (stock picking) accounts for about 5%, and digressing from the ideal asset allocation to take into account outside influences on the markets (market timing) accounts for about 2%.

A number of factors go into determining your optimal asset allocation, including

- your age;
- your health;
- whether or not you need income from your portfolio; and
- changing life events (divorce, death of a spouse, loss of a job).

Remember this general rule: The larger the percentage of stocks in your portfolio, the greater the risk. It is also important to appreciate the differences in the upside and downside potential of a very conservative and a very risky portfolio.

For example, for the 29-year period ending in 2005, a very conservative portfolio consisting entirely of intermediate-term bonds would have had an annualized return of 9.3% and a worst 12-month loss of 4.5%.

At the other end of the spectrum, an all-Canadian stock portfolio during the same time period would have had an annualized return of 11.7% and a worst 12-month loss of 15.1%.

Ignoring your cash requirements (which financial planners suggest should amount to six months to one year of living expenses), almost all investors should have an asset allocation somewhere between these two extremes.

There are all kinds of formulas for figuring out your proper asset allocation. The most common rule of thumb is to take your age and subtract it from 100. The answer is the percent of your portfolio that should be in stocks. So, as you get older you should have more of your portfolio in bonds (e.g., a 30-year-old should have 70/30 in stocks/bonds, while her 60-year-old mother should have 40/60 in stocks/bonds).

I find this formula too simplistic to be of any real use because it fails to take into account the many variables among investors of the same age (such as health and income) that could make the results of this formula very misleading. However, it is still better than the practice of many hyperactive brokers and advisors, which is to place 90% or more of their clients' assets in stocks.

There are also all kinds of questionnaires available on the internet that you can fill out to determine your optimal asset allocation. Many of them suffer from oversimplification and are really not of much value.

I have prepared a questionnaire for those of you who want to validate your asset allocation decision (see Appendix A). While it is not uncomplicated, you should be able to fill it out in about 15 minutes.

A much easier and even quicker way to use this questionnaire is to go to the website for this book, www.smartest
investmentbook.com—a site that is programmed to be interactive, with all of the calculations performed automatically.

While no questionnaire, including the one in this book,
should be the only source you rely on to determine your asset
allocation, my questionnaire is a reliable guide to helping you
find the right asset allocation *for you*.

But in the interest of keeping things simple, let me say this:
Most individuals would be well advised to use one of the
following four portfolios (in ascending order of risk):

- low risk
- medium-low risk
- medium-high risk
- high risk

In order to decide which of these portfolios is the right one
for you, you need to understand the long-term history of the
returns and the risks associated with each portfolio. In doing
so, remember that the future performance may not be the
same as these historical numbers. But this is the most reliable
data available to us.

You can do this quite easily by taking another look at the
chart on page 125, which I showed you earlier in Chapter 4.

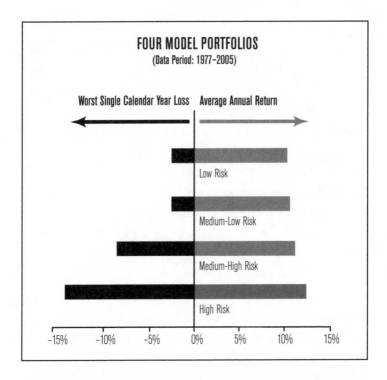

FOUR MODEL PORTFOLIOS
(Data Period: 1977–2005)

Worst Single Calendar Year Loss   Average Annual Return

Low Risk

Medium-Low Risk

Medium-High Risk

High Risk

-15%   -10%   -5%   0%   5%   10%   15%

Let's start with the riskiest of these four portfolios, which is the high-risk portfolio. That portfolio returned an average 12.15% during this time period. In its worst 12-month period, it lost 13.95%.

If those kinds of losses in your portfolio would cause you undue concern, then this portfolio is too risky for you.

Now let's go down one level of risk and look at the medium-high-risk portfolio. That portfolio returned an average of 11.56% during the same period. This return is 0.59% less than the high-risk portfolio. But in its worst 12-month period, it lost only 7.99% (5.96% less than the high-risk portfolio).

I don't mean to downplay the significance of a 0.59% difference in returns. Over a 20-year period, that could mean a difference of $99,200 on an initial investment of $100,000.

Now let's go down one more level of risk and look at the medium-low-risk portfolio. The annualized returns were 10.89%. Its worst single calendar year was a loss of 2.02%. This is certainly a far less risky portfolio than the medium-high-risk portfolio.

Is this difference in returns worth the significant additional downside risk to you? If not, then you should seriously consider the medium-low-risk portfolio.

Now let's look at the most conservative of these four portfolios, the low-risk portfolio. The annualized returns for this very stable portfolio were 10.14%. Its worst single calendar year was a loss of 2.07%. At first blush, this portfolio actually seems riskier that the medium-low-risk portfolio because its worst single calendar year loss is slightly greater than the loss of that portfolio. However, if you refer to Appendix B, you will see that the worst two- and three-year periods for this portfolio are very significantly superior to those in the medium-low-risk portfolio. And the standard deviation of this portfolio is slightly less. When this data is considered, it is clear that this portfolio is less risky than the medium-low-risk portfolio.

Are you comfortable with historical annualized returns of 10.14%? If so, why would you want to assume more risk? If not, you should consider one of the other three higher-risk portfolios.

If hyperactive brokers and advisors presented data this way, most investors would have no problem figuring out what asset allocation was appropriate for them. But brokers and advisors rarely do.

Now you should have an asset allocation that is suitable for you. The most difficult part of this process—the most critical part—is done.

Chapter 35

Step 2: Open a Brokerage Account and Purchase ETFs

ETFs are excellent investment tools that can provide instant diversification beyond traditional stocks and mutual funds; and boast the additional advantages of being low cost, transparent, and, simply, a convenient way to invest.

—Howard J. Atkinson, head of public funds, Barclays Global Investors Canada Limited, *Indexing Made Easy—A Look at Popular Investing Strategies Using ETFs*. Reported at: https://www.bmoinvestorline.com/EducationCentre/ETF/ ETFSpecialReportEN.pdf#search='ETFs%20Canada%20 excellent%20investment

ETFs are mutual fund-like products that trade on an organized stock exchange, like the Toronto Stock Exchange in Canada and the American Stock Exchange in the United States. ETFs are frequently designed to replicate the returns of a particular index, like the TSE 300 Index and many others.

Because ETFs trade on an exchange, they can be traded at any time during the day that the exchange is open for business. In addition, the fees charged by ETFs are very low, which makes them a reasonable alternative to index funds.

However, there are some disadvantages to ETFs. Since ETFs trade like stocks, you have to open a brokerage account to trade them. They also incur commissions like stocks. You will pay these commissions when you initially invest your portfolio, when you add to your investment portfolio and when you rebalance your portfolio.

There is increasing competition in Canada among discount brokerage firms eager for your business. Some are offering trades as low as $9.99 and do not charge anything for account maintenance. It is important to find a low-cost firm to execute these trades. Otherwise, the cost of the transactions and the minimum charges applied by some firms could significantly reduce the returns to investors with less than $50,000 to invest.

I recommend that Canadian investors use ETFs to become Smart Investors.

Chapter 36

Step 3: Select Your Investments

Surprisingly, one-third of all index funds carry either front-end or asset-based sales charges. Why an investor would opt to pay a commission on an index fund when a substantially identical fund is available without a commission remains a mystery.
—John C. Bogle, *Common Sense on Mutual Funds*

This step is the easy part.

All we know about the stock and bond markets is that over time both will go up in value.

As I have explained, no one can predict which stock or which bond will increase in value, or when it will increase. And no one will know when or by how much the entire market will increase in value.

Therefore, investors should own the entire market. By the "entire market," I mean a broadly diversified portfolio of investments in domestic and international markets.

Let's take another look at the chart on the following page that I showed you in Chapter 4. It tells you precisely which

ETFs to select, and what percentage of your portfolio should be invested in each ETF, depending on the portfolio you have selected.

COMPOSITION OF FOUR MODEL PORTFOLIOS

FUND NAME	LOW RISK	MEDIUM-LOW RISK	MEDIUM-HIGH RISK	HIGH RISK
iShares CDN Composite Index Fund (XIC)	2%	4%	6%	8%
iShares CDN S&P 500 Index Fund (XSP)	10%	20%	30%	40%
iShares CDN MSCI EAFE Index Fund (XIN)	8%	16%	24%	32%
iShares CDN Bond Index Fund (XBB)	80%	60%	40%	20%
	100%	100%	100%	100%

As you will note, I recommend that, for each of these portfolios, you take the total amount of the assets you will be investing in stock funds, and invest 10% of that amount in a Canadian stock fund and the balance in foreign stocks. There is strong academic evidence that portfolios with exposure to foreign markets have similar historical returns, *but less risk,* than portfolios invested only in the domestic stock market. This is particularly important for Canadian investors, because Canadian stocks constitute less than 3% of the market value of the world's equities. Canadian investors who are overweighed in Canadian equities are missing out on opportunities to improve their returns, while minimizing the risk of having all of their equity eggs in a basket that depends on the variable fortunes of one country.

Want specifics?

For the 25-year period ending December 31, 2000, a portfolio invested 100% in stocks in the TSE 300 Index yielded a return of 13.7%, with a risk measured by standard deviation of 16.8%.

However, for the same period, an investment of 80% in an index of world stocks (the MSCI World Index), and only 20% in the TSE 300 Index, had a *higher* return of 16.7%, with a *lower* risk of 13.2%.

Canadian Smart Investors need to broaden their investment horizons.

Chapter 37

Step 4: Rebalance Your Portfolio

Active management is little more than a gigantic con game.
—Ron Ross, Ph.D., *The Unbeatable Market*

Nothing is more important than your asset allocation. Therefore, it is important that your allocation remain where you want it to be.

But markets are inherently volatile, and the values of the individual investments constantly change. This means that every day your asset allocation drifts away from or closer to the original allocation you set.

Stocks and bonds may change value in opposition to one another. As bonds become more valuable, stocks may become less valuable, and vice versa. Over short periods of time, nobody can predict which way stocks and bonds will move or whether they will move together or in opposition. However, over the long run, stocks have returned more than bonds.

Over the course of six months, a lot can happen in the markets, and your investments in both stocks and bonds can drift quite a bit away from your initial asset allocation. An original 60/40 stock-to-bond allocation could be 45/55 stock-to-bond after six months if the value of stocks falls dramatically, or 75/25 if the value of stocks rises dramatically. Hence the need to rebalance.

Rebalancing can also be necessary because some life event has changed your need for income from your portfolio or your sense of how much risk you can assume in your portfolio.

There are two ways to rebalance your portfolio: If you have an opportunity to add new money to your portfolio, you can buy more of the assets that you need to rebalance the portfolio. If you must work only with the assets you currently have, you need to sell some of the assets that are over-represented in the portfolio and buy more of the assets that are under-represented.

For instance, if your medium-high-risk portfolio now has 55% of its value in stocks and 45% in bonds, you are under-represented in stocks and over-represented in bonds.

Whatever the reason for your rebalancing, it should take you only 45 minutes or so, twice a year, to complete the exercise, since you will be dealing with only a small number of ETFs.

If you use an investment advisor, he or she should call you up every six months or so to go over your portfolio, determine if there is any reason to change your asset allocation, then perform the necessary transactions for you to rebalance the portfolio.

Chapter 38

What About Income Trusts?

The current income-trust boom has striking similarities to the tech bubble of 1999 and 2000.
—Dirk Zetzsche, Ph.D., "The Need for Regulating Income Trusts: A Bubble Theory," *University of Toronto Law Review,* vol. 63, no. 1, 2005

Canadian investors love income trusts. There are currently more than 300 income trusts listed on Canadian exchanges, with a market capitalization in excess of $180 billion.

What are **income trusts** (also known as income funds)? They are investments in qualified businesses that distribute most of their earnings to investors each month or quarter. These distributions are generally higher than dividends from non-qualified corporations because the income distributed has not been subject to corporate tax.

> **INCOME TRUSTS** are investments in qualified businesses that distribute most of their earnings to investors each month or quarter.

However, continued exemption from tax on the earnings of income trusts is currently subject to review by the federal government in Ottawa, a situation that has created great uncertainty in this sector in Canada.

The track record of income trusts is too brief to draw any meaningful conclusions about them. I reviewed the performance of all of the income trusts that had a minimum three-year track record as of May 31, 2006. There were only 30 of them. Of these, only 12 (40%) beat the returns of the S&P/TSX Composite Index during that time period. The management expense ratio of these funds was an average of 2.28%, which is roughly comparable to the expense ratio of Canadian actively managed mutual funds and significantly higher than the ETFs in my recommended portfolios.

Given the uncertainty over the tax status of these trusts, their modest track record and the high cost of owning them, it is difficult to understand the enthusiasm of Canadian investors for these investments.

Smart Investors who believe that income trusts should nevertheless be included in their portfolios might want to consider iShares CDN Income Trust Sector Index Fund. This ETF replicates the performance of the income trust issuers listed on the Toronto Stock Exchange. Its management expense ratio is 0.55%, which adds another layer of fees to the 2.28% charged on average by actively managed income trusts. However, ownership of this ETF would relieve Smart Investors from the onerous—if not impossible—task of picking "winners" from the vast number of income trusts that have recently proliferated in Canada.

Chapter 39

Don't Back Down

Wall Street's favourite scam is pretending that luck is skill.
—Ron Ross, Ph.D., *The Unbeatable Market*

Now that you have decided to reject Hyperactive Investing and become a Smart Investor, you need to be able to face your hyperactive broker or investment advisor. They are a hard-nosed bunch, with the thick skin necessary to be good salespeople. They have been rejected hundreds of times before, and have been trained to have a response to any objection a potential client could serve up.

So here are a few tips on how to face them down.

When you confront your hyperactive broker or advisor with the overwhelming evidence to support your desire to become a Smart Investor, you will hear some variation of one or more of the following responses:

- There is no "alpha" (meaning no value added) when you just invest for market returns.
- Smart Investing is for conservative investors only.
- We can pick stocks and time the market, or give your money to the top advisors who can.

Your response—assuming you feel the need to give one—should consist of some variation of one or more of the following:

- Being a Smart Investor will consistently give me the same returns as the market in general, less any applicable fees. There is overwhelming evidence that being a Hyperactive Investor will give me inconsistent returns. While some years I may beat the market, other years I will not. Over the long term, my cumulative returns as a Hyperactive Investor will be less than the market, especially when I consider the high fees, taxes and other costs involved.
- Being a Smart Investor is appropriate for both conservative and aggressive investors. What determines how conservative or aggressive I am is my asset allocation, not whether I am, or am not, trying to beat the markets. There are ways to invest in more aggressive markets (by increasing the percentage of stocks in my portfolio, for example) that can be extremely aggressive but still produce the market returns for that market and, when owned in the correct proportion within my portfolio, do not add undue risk.
- You may be able to show me some short-term results, where a particular money manager has beaten the market three or five years running. But, over the long term, I will outperform the vast majority of mutual funds by being a Smart Investor, since academic research shows that there is no way to predict which mutual funds will perform well, and which ones will not, in the future.

Instead of just being on the defensive, ask your hyperactive broker or advisor these questions:

1. What is my asset allocation?

   If it is more than 80% stocks, and even if it is less than that, it may be too risky for you.

2. What is my standard deviation?

   If it is more than 30%, and even if it is significantly less than that, it may be too risky for you.

3. Are you acting as a fiduciary in your dealings with me, which requires you to act solely in my best interest? If not, why won't you agree to do so?

   If he or she will not agree to act solely in your best interest, you should not do business with this advisor.

4. Do you engage in market timing and stock picking? What facts do you have that indicate that you or anyone else can do this successfully over the long term?

   If your advisor engages in market timing or stock picking, he or she is gambling with your money. What does he or she know that Smart Investors, who account for 76% of all trades in the U.S. markets, don't? Why are you part of the disadvantaged minority?

5. Why wouldn't I be better off investing in a suitably allocated portfolio of exchange-traded funds, with much lower expense ratios, than in actively managed mutual funds, over the long term?

   If your advisor says anything other than "You would," he or she either does not understand the data or is not being candid with you.

Then walk out the door, close your account and become a Smart Investor.

Chapter 40

Where Are the Pension Plans for Smart Investors?

[A]ctive investment management is a source of pension fund losses, not profits. Individual funds can have profitable strategies, but aggregate profits are negative because of manager fees and transactions costs. The recent growth in passive investment products and increased interest in performance-linked fees are evidence that Canada's pension community recognizes how difficult it is to earn above-market returns.

—John Ilkiw, "Pension Fund Financing: A Plan Sponsor's Guide to Fiduciary Duty." Reported at: http://www.benefits canada.com/content/legacy/Content/1997/03-97/f1.html

For many Canadian investors, their registered pension plans (RPPs) and their Registered Retirement Savings Plans (**RRSPs**) represent an important part of their retirement planning. However, it can be very difficult to be a Smart Investor in many of these plans.

An **RRSP** is a savings plan for individuals that allows them to defer paying tax on money to be used for retirement.

Frequently, investment managers or financial advisors are retained to advise on the investment of RPP and RRSP assets. If these investment managers or advisors are hyperactive, they are not incentivized to recommend low-cost ETFs. This bias deprives Smart Investors of the superior returns and lower costs offered by ETFs.

Of course, if you have a self-directed RRSP, using an online broker, you can invest in the same portfolio of ETFs that you have selected for the balance of your investible assets.

If you find that there are no (or few) ETFs or index fund investments in your pension plan, complain to the person responsible for selecting the investment managers of the plan. If there are enough complaints, you will start to see investment options for these plans that will permit the beneficiaries to become Smart Investors.

Chapter 41

Have the Inmates Taken Over the Asylum?

Of course. I favour passive investing for most investors, because markets are amazingly successful devices for incorporating information into stock prices. I believe, along with Friedrich Hayek [a Nobel laureate, and a contemporary of John Maynard Keynes] and others, that information is not some big thing that's locked in a safe somewhere. It exists in bits and pieces scattered all over the world.

—Merton Miller, Nobel laureate in economics, "An Interview with Merton Miller," by Peter Tanous, *Investment Gurus,* February 1997

The securities industries in both Canada and the United States are among the most heavily regulated industries in the world. The question is: Who is being protected?

Merton Miller, who won the Nobel Prize in Economic Sciences in 1990, was of the view that the principal beneficiary of securities regulation in the United States was the securities industry. He was a strong proponent of passive investing, as indicated by the quotation that begins this chapter.

It has been suggested that the same observation may be applied to the relationship between the Ontario Securities Commission and the securities industry it regulates (together with provincial regulators) in Canada.

Can this be accurate?

The highly regarded financial author, William Bernstein, wrote:

> Then again, there is a third type of investor—the investment professional, who indeed knows that he or she doesn't know, but whose livelihood depends upon appearing to know.

Every day, financial advisors in Canada and the United States tell investors that they can beat the markets or that they can time the markets, or that a particular stock is "underpriced" or that a particular mutual fund is "hot." The overwhelming academic evidence is that these statements have precious little to back them up.

Investors who have relied on this advice have lost billions of dollars.

There is a dizzying array of regulations governing the financial services industry. Why are there none that require brokers and advisors who profess to be able to beat the markets to disclose the compelling evidence of their inability to do so?

Investors who wished to ignore this information would still be free to buy into the sales pitch of their advisors. But at least they would be fully informed before taking the plunge.

Have the wolves of Bay Street and Wall Street devoured the regulatory lambs in Toronto and Washington?

The Smartest Investor Who Ever Read an Investment Book

Some people change their minds because they want to, others because they have to.
—Howard Gardner, *Changing Minds*

Hyperactive brokers and advisors have a vested interest in convincing you that investing is terribly complex and certainly not something you can undertake on your own. Their agenda is to drive you to use them, so that they can convince you of how they can beat the markets and, by the way, generate fees for themselves and their firms.

If you have read this far, you know that this is not true. These advisors are clinging to a discredited, minority practice, hoping that you will be too confused or distracted to find out that you are part of the disadvantaged, declining minority of investors buying into their "professional advice."

You can take control of your own investments with minimal time and effort—and by doing so you are likely to outperform the vast majority of these "investment professionals."

Specifically, this is what you now appreciate:

1. The single greatest threat to your financial well-being is the hyperactive broker or advisor.
2. The second greatest threat to your financial well-being is the false belief that you can trade on your own, online or otherwise, and attempt to beat the markets by engaging in stock picking or market timing.
3. The third greatest threat to your financial well-being is paying attention to much of the financial media, which is often engaged in nothing more than "financial pornography." This conduct generates advertising revenues for these media, and losses for investors who rely on the misinformation that is their daily grist.
4. Depending on the amount of risk you are willing to assume, as a Smart Investor, it is reasonable to expect your portfolio to achieve annualized returns ranging from 10% to 12% over the long term. Attempting to achieve returns higher than 15% involves speculating. If you decide to speculate, you understand that you are assuming a significantly increased risk of losing all, or a substantial portion, of your assets.
5. If you choose one of the four portfolios I have described, and invest in the ETFs I have specified, you are likely to beat the returns of 95% of actively managed mutual funds over the long term.

Now relax and enjoy your life, secure in the knowledge that you have provided as best you can for yourself and your family.

You are now the smartest investor who has ever read an investment book!

Chapter 43

Too Good to Be True?

So who still believes markets don't work? Apparently it is only the North Koreans, the Cubans and the active managers.
—"Active vs. Passive Management," transcript of Rex Sinquefield's opening statement in debate with Donald Yacktman at the Schwab Institutional conference in San Francisco, October 12, 1995. Reported at: http://library.dfaus.com/articles/active_vs_passive

You know the old adage: If something sounds too good to be true, it probably is. This does not apply here.

People are always throwing around statistics and studies to support whatever they are selling. How do you know if what they are saying (or writing) really is true?

When it comes to providing support for avoiding hyperactive advisors and brokers and adopting the investment strategies I have set forth, there is an overwhelming amount of data. For those of you who want to do additional research to verify the statements made in this book, the underlying authority is presented on the pages that follow, but it by no means is intended to be an exhaustive listing of every study on this subject. I have organized it by chapter.

Since this is really a bibliography, which I know can be tedious and boring, those of you who are already convinced and need no further support can skip this chapter.

Chapter 1: An Unbelievable Chimp Story

Information about the *Financial Times* contest was reported in the *Sunday Mail* (Queensland, Australia), March 17, 2002.

Commenting on her stunning victory over the highly credentialled "independent analyst," the five-year-old, Tia Roberts, thought it was "wicked."

She has a point there.

Studies that show the merit, or lack of merit, of analyst recommendations are nicely summarized in a paper entitled "An Empirical Model of Stock Analysts' Recommendations: Market Fundamentals, Conflicts of Interest, and Peer Effects," written by Patrick Bajari and John Krainer. You can find this paper online at http://ideas.repec.org/p/nbr/nberwo/10665.html.

Chapter 2: An Unbelievable True Story

An article written by Jonathan Chevreau in the *Financial Post* on November 5, 2005, stated that $554 billion was invested in all mutual funds in Canada as of September 2005. Of that amount, $124 million was invested in Canadian equity funds. See http://www.canada.com/national/nationalpost/financial post/fpweekend/story.html?id=fc98997b-10cf-4b0b-9bb1-5d900bf907bf.

The Investment Funds Institute of Canada is an excellent source for information concerning mutual funds in Canada. As of July 5, 2005, it indicated that $591 billion was invested in mutual funds in Canada. See http://www.ific.ca/eng/home/index.asp.

I rely in part on a speech by John Bogle, entitled "As the Index Fund Moves from Heresy to Dogma ... What More Do We Need to Know?" (the Gary M. Brinson Distinguished Lecture, April 13, 2004), for the data indicating the historical underperformance of actively managed funds when compared with index funds, primarily caused by the increased costs of the actively managed funds. See http://www.vanguard.com/bogle_site/sp20040413.html.

For details concerning the hundreds of millions of advertising dollars spent every year by brokerage firms, see http://www.onwallstreet.com/article.cfm?articleId=2401.

After all, it is not easy to convince you to buy an expertise they don't have!

Chapter 3: Smart Investing Takes Less Time Than Brunch

There is no better compendium of the hundreds of studies demonstrating the underperformance of active management than the database found at the website of Index Funds Advisors: http://www.ifa.com/library/articledatabase.asp.

Great credit should be given to Mark Hebner, president of Index Funds Advisors, for this excellent website, which is an extremely valuable resource.

The June 26, 2002, issue of the *Christian Science Monitor* reported that stock market losses aggregated about $5.5 trillion in the prior 27 months "or nearly three times what the U.S. government spends annually."

There are many studies that show that the vast majority of actively managed mutual funds fail to beat their benchmark over the long term. See "Will Active Mutual Funds Continue to Underperform the Market in the Future?" by John Bogle, in Scott Simon's book *Index Mutual Funds: Profiting from an Investment Revolution;* see also the article by Edward S. O'Neal, discussed in Chapter 13, and a study by Dalbar, Inc., a well-respected research firm. Reported at http://www.dalbarinc.com/content/showpage.asp?page=2001062100.

Burton Malkiel summarizes these studies in *A Random Walk Down Wall Street,* p. 187.

In Mark Hebner's book, *Index Funds: The 12-Step Program for Active Investors* (pp. 47–53), he sets forth the studies showing the lack of consistency of mutual fund performance and the daunting odds of picking an actively managed fund that will outperform its benchmark index.

One particularly compelling study referenced by Hebner indicated that, for the 10-year period ending October 2004, only 2.4% of the 1446 funds that had as a goal beating the S&P 500 Index succeeded in doing so.

Chapter 4: Drop Me to the Bottom Line

For a helpful and informative article on the use of ETFs in Canada, see an article by Howard J. Atkinson, "Indexing Made Easy—A Look at Popular Investing Strategies Using ETFs." Mr. Atkinson is the head of public funds at Barclays Global Investors Canada Limited. The article is available online at

https://www.bmoinvestorline.com/EducationCentre/ETF/
ETFSpecialReportEN.pdf#search='ETFs%20Canada.

Chapter 5: Smart Investing Simply Makes Sense

The study demonstrating the decline of stock picking in the United States is Utpal Bhattacharya and Neal E. Galpin's "Is Stock Picking Declining Around the World?" (November 2005). It is available at http://papers.ssrn.com/sol3/papers.cfm?abstract_id=849627.

The study showing that investors who selected their own mutual funds outperformed the funds sold by financial advisors, including brokers, is Daniel B. Bergstresser, John M.R. Chalmers, and Peter Tufano's "Assessing the Costs and Benefits of Brokers in the Mutual Fund Industry" (January 16, 2006). It is available at: http://ssrn.com/abstract=616981.

The well-credentialled and highly respected authors of this study performed an analysis of the cost and performance of more than 4000 mutual funds sold by financial advisors and selected by investors from 1996 to 2002. Here is what they found:

- Funds selected by financial advisors significantly *under-performed* those selected by investors on their own. The risk-adjusted returns were *lower.*
- Funds selected by advisors were *higher cost* than those selected by investors on their own.
- Advisors did *not* provide superior asset allocation to their clients.

- Advisors did *not* prevent their clients from pursuing ill-advised investor behaviour, like chasing performance.

You have to ask yourself, given these findings, why you would rely on these "investment professionals" for financial advice. It is bad enough that they do not *add* value. This study demonstrates that they in fact *subtract* value.

Chapter 6: Brokers Make Money When They Are Hyperactive

The data for the performance of funds from 1945 to 1974 comes from the Bogle speech referred to in the notes to Chapter 2, above.

There is an excellent discussion of the excessive costs of hyperactive funds and their adverse effect on returns in Mark Hebner's exhaustive book, *Index Funds: The 12-Step Program for Active Investors,* pp. 126–130.

Pay particular attention to the discussion of the effect of taxes that can cause investors to lose over 50% of their cumulative returns in the average hyperactively managed fund.

In contrast, investors in index funds lose only 13% of returns over the same (15-year) period.

The bottom line is that index funds and ETFs are far more tax-efficient than hyperactive funds, which is another compelling reason to avoid hyperactive funds.

The studies that demonstrate that actively managed funds in Canada underperform their benchmarks over the long term are nicely summarized by Richard Deaves, Ph.D., in his informative book *What Kind of an Investor Are You?* (pp. 103–109). The studies are specifically cited at pp. 109–110. Another study that reaches the same conclusion is one authored by Rajeeva Sinha, professor of finance, Odette School of Business, University of Windsor, and Vijay M. Jog, professor of finance, Eric Sprott School of Business, Carleton University, August 17, 2004, a copy of which was kindly provided to me by the authors.

Chapter 7: A Loser's Game

The study indicating that the average equity fund investor had an annualized return of 3.7% for the 20-year period from 1985 to 2004, when the S&P returned 13.2%, is a 2005 study prepared by Dalbar, Inc. An updated study by Dalbar found that investors who simply held on to an S&P 500 index fund for the past 20 years would have earned an 11.9% annual return.

What kind of returns did the average investor, guided by his or her "investment professional," actually achieve? A pathetic 3.9%. The study is reported in the June 26, 2006, edition of *BusinessWeek Online,* available at http://www.business week.com/magazine/content/06_26/b3990104.htm?chan= investing_investing+funds.

The data for the actual versus reported returns of the Fidelity Aggressive Growth Fund is derived from a study attributed to Charles Trzcinka, professor of finance at the University of Indiana, and reported in Mark Hebner's book, *Index Funds: The 12-Step Program for Active Investors,* p. 10.

Chapter 8: Why Investors Pursue Hyperactive Investing

According to an article in *OWS Magazine,* December 2003, Wall Street firms spent *$428 million* in advertising in 2000. The misleading claims in this advertising onslaught are rarely challenged in either paid advertising or editorial comment. No wonder there are so many Hyperactive Investors and so few Smart Investors!

An article about the entry of U.S. brokers into "Canada's staid securities industry," entitled "U.S. Brokers Boost Stock in Canada," by John Gray, appeared in *Strategy Magazine* on March 29, 1999. It can be found at http://www.strategy mag.com/articles/magazine/19990329/25054.html.

There are many studies in behavioural finance that support the statements in this chapter, which describes the reasons why investors continue to ignore the data and continue to be Hyperactive Investors. An excellent summary of this research can be found at http://www.investorhome.com/psych.htm. There are useful hyperlinks there to the underlying research.

Exhaustive information about "hot hand" research can be found at http://thehothand.blogspot.com.

The reprehensible conduct of hyperactive funds touting the "sizzle" of their past performance was recently exposed by the outstanding journalist Jonathan Clements of the *Wall Street Journal,* in an online column entitled "Those Performance-Touting Fund Ads Are Back—And That Could Mean Trouble." It is summarized at: http://socialize.morningstar.com/New Socialize/asp/FullConv.asp?forumId=F100000015&lastConv Seq=41356 . Clements is the rare exception to those financial journalists who routinely peddle "financial pornography."

Here is what Burton Malkiel has to say about charting (which he likens to "alchemy") in his seminal book, *A Random Walk Down Wall Street,* (p. 165): "There has been a remarkable uniformity in the conclusions of studies done on all forms of technical analysis. Not one has consistently outperformed the placebo of a buy-and-hold strategy. Technical methods cannot be used to make useful investment strategies."

Malkiel believes that chartists simply provide cover for hyperactive brokers to encourage more trading—generating more fees—by their unsuspecting clients.

It is noteworthy that, in February 2005, Citigroup fired its entire technical analysis group. This was reported at http://www.shiaustreet.com/2005/february/18/ta.php.

If you are *really* interested in this subject, here are three articles that challenge the usefulness of technical analysis:

1. Fama and Blume. "Filter Rules and Stock Market Trading Profits." *Journal of Business,* Special Supplement, January 1966, 226–241.
2. Jensen and Benington. "Random Walks and Technical Theories: Some Additional Evidence." *Journal of Finance,* May 1970, 469–482.
3. Ball. "Filter Rules: Interpretation of Market Efficiency, Experimental Problem and Australian Experience." *Accounting Education,* November 1978, 1–7.

The study on the relationship between speculative investors in Ontario and gambling is: "An Analysis of Self-identified Speculative Investors," by Richard Govoni, Robert E. Mann and Harold Wynne, *Journal of Gambling Issues,* July 2004. It is available at http://www.camh.net/egambling/issue11/jgi_11_govoni_mann_wynne.html.

The study found that more speculative investors who were gamblers fell into higher risk categories of gamblers than those from the gambling population at large. By extrapolating data from the group sampled, the study theorized that there are approximately 456,000 people in Ontario who are "self-identified speculative investors and gamblers." Of this group, 9576 would be considered "severe problem gamblers" and 37,848 would be "moderate problem" gamblers.

These numbers are troublesome.

Chapter 9: The "Activity" Myth

The seminal study on the adverse effects of trading costs on profitability is entitled "Trading Is Hazardous to Your Wealth: The Common Stock Investment Performance of Individual Investors." It was published in *The Journal of Finance* (vol. 4, no. 2. April 2000) and co-authored by Barber and Odean. This impressive study conclusively demonstrated a negative correlation between the amount of trading and profitability. This is not surprising.

By definition, hyperactive brokers and advisors encourage their clients to engage in more trading than investors need to do if they are simply seeking market returns. And hyperactive funds trade more than index funds. This increased amount of trading contributes significantly to the underperformance of these actively trading investors and funds.

Chapter 11: Brokers Aren't on Your Side

The study of analyst ratings for firms that went bankrupt in 2002 was done by Weiss Ratings, Inc. It was reported in a speech given to the National Press Club on June 11, 2002, entitled "Crisis of Confidence on Wall Street." You can access this speech, which contains far more details about this study, at http://www.weissratings.com/crisis_of_confidence.asp.

Details of the US$1.4-billion settlement with major brokerage firms involving allegations of analyst fraud may be found at http://www.sec.gov/news/press/2002-179.htm.

Chapter 12: Hyperactive Brokers, Underachieving Students

John J. De Goey is a senior financial advisor with Assante Capital Management Ltd., and author of *The Professional Financial Advisor*, Insomniac Press (January 2004). Mr. De Goey is a crusader for full disclosure and a powerful advocate for investors in Canada. In addition to the quotation at the beginning of this chapter, he stated the following in his submission to Finance Canada's 2006 Review of Financial Sector Legislation:

There is considerable academic evidence that active management (stock picking and fund picking) is not a value-adding proposition. In a large majority of cases, this activity fails to add value. Most advisors are unaware of this fact because they have never been taught about the comparative merits of active and passive strategies. Poor training leads to poor advice, and the advice most consumers receive is tantamount to unsubstantiated, industry-specific folklore.

His full submission is available at http://www.fin.gc.ca/consultresp/06Rev_12e.html.

Chapter 13: What Do You Think of These Odds?

The cited study by Edward O'Neal was a private study that was provided to me by the author.

The private study of Canadian mutual funds was done with Sean Kelly, a principal of Kelly & Associates, West Palm Beach, Florida.

I have previously referenced the studies done by others that reached the same, or similar, conclusions. See the notes to Chapter 6, above.

Chapter 14: Nobody Can Time the Market

The study on market-timing newsletters was performed by two researchers at Duke University and the University of Utah ("National Bureau of Economic Research Working Paper 4890") and published in another form in the *Journal of Financial Economics,* vol. 42, 1996, pp. 397–421.

Other studies have also debunked the myth of market timing. A very compelling one was authored by John D. Stowe, and is aptly entitled "A Market Timing Myth" (*Journal of Investing*, Winter, 2000).

Alan Greenspan first used the term *irrational exuberance* in a speech entitled "The Challenge of Central Banking in a Democratic Society" on December 5, 1996, before the American Enterprise Institute for Public Policy Research in Washington, D.C.

Chapter 15: Nobody Can Consistently Beat the Market

For an interesting study that discusses how trading costs can basically negate the value of analyst recommendations, see "Can Investors Profit from the Prophets? Security Analyst Recommendations and Stock Returns," by Brad Barber, Reuvan Lehavy, Maureen McNichols and Brett Trueman, Graduate School of Business, Stanford University, available at https://gsbapps.stanford.edu/researchpapers/Library/RP1541. pdf#search='analyst%20recommendations%20under perform%20market.

The study by Patrick Bajari and John Krainer is "An Empirical Model of Stock Analysts' Recommendations: Market Fundamentals, Conflicts of Interest, and Peer Effects." This paper is available at http://ideas.repec.org/p/nbr/nberwo/10665.html.

Chapter 16: Nobody Can Pick "Hot" Fund Managers

The short holding periods of investors in hyperactively traded mutual funds has been noted in a series of private studies done by Dalbar, Inc. A summary of these studies can be found at: http://www.latrobefinancialmanagement.com/2006%20 Research%20PDF/Chasing%20Mutual%20Fund%20Investors %20Earn%20Less%20Inflation.pdf.

This quest for the outperforming "hot" funds is obviously counterproductive. It only exacerbates the already dismal odds against finding any hyperactively managed mutual fund that will outperform a comparable index fund.

The data on the lack of correlation between the Morningstar five-star ratings and future performance is set forth in a study co-authored by Christopher R. Blake and Matthew R. Morey, entitled "Morningstar Ratings and Mutual Fund Performance," December 22, 1999, available at http://www.bnet.fordham.edu/public/finance/cblake/ mstarv2a.pdf#search='Morey%20Blake%20Morningstar.

Another study noted that funds selected by Morningstar for its own 401(k) plan significantly underperformed a broad U.S.-market index for the period 1991 to 1999. The same study found that top-performing mutual funds selected by *Forbes,* the *New York Times, Worth* magazine, *BusinessWeek* and 59 investment newsletters studied over a 10-year period all underperformed the same index. See Ravi Agrawal, "Active vs. Passive Investing," *A Research Review,* April 2004.

An interesting study looked at the 25 mutual funds selected by *USA Today* and designated as "all-stars" because of their supposed ability to be long-term winners. The study found no evidence that these "all-star" funds produced superior returns in the years after their initial selection. See Stanley M. Atkinson and Ray R. Sturm, "All-Star Mutual Funds?" *Journal of Investing,* vol. 12, no. 2, Summer, 2003.

There is a reason why mutual funds are required to state that "past performance is not indicative of future results"!

Morningstar Canada makes its fund star rating of Canadian mutual funds available to investors at http://www.morning star.ca/globalhome/industry/fundtable.asp?quick=basic&star rating5=5&nodata=0.

Many investors continue to believe that "five-star" ratings by Morningstar of mutual funds available to Canadian investors are somehow predictive of future performance.

They aren't.

Chapter 17: Why Recommend This Mutual Fund?

The fees paid by purchasers of actively managed mutual funds in Canada are fully described on the website of the Investment Funds Institute of Canada, available at http://www.ific.ca/pdf/ investorFAQ/Mutual_Fund_Fees.pdf#search='Investment% 20Funds%20Institute%20of%20Canada%20Mutual% 20Fund%20Fees.

However, the fees noted by this industry organization do not necessarily represent all of the fees that should concern investors. In a speech to the Bullseye 2000 conference held in Toronto on December 4, 2000, John Bogle, the founder of the Vanguard Group, calculated the "real" fees of the average actively managed fund in Canada at a staggering 5.7%! The full text of this sobering and informative speech is available at http://www.vanguard.com/bogle_site/december042000.html.

Chapter 18: Hyperactive Investing Is Expensive

Information on the high cost of actively managed funds compared with index funds is set forth in the Bogle speech referenced in the notes to Chapter 2.

The support for the discussion of the tax consequences of investing in hyperactive funds is set forth in the notes to Chapter 6.

An informative lament on the difference between fees charged for active and passive mutual funds in Canada and the United States, and the barriers imposed by the Ontario Securities Commission to access to U.S. brokerage firms by Canadian investors, is set forth in an article entitled "Buying [Past Tense] US Mutual Funds and Stocks from Canada." It is available at http://www.bylo.org/usmfcan.html.

A very complete article setting forth the details of the excessive fees paid by Canadian investors for equity mutual funds (aggregating $10 billion in 2002), and the deleterious effects these fees have on fund performance, may be found in an article entitled "What Canadians Pay for Fund Management," by Mark Warywoda, June 10, 2003. It is available at http://www.morningstar.ca/globalhome/Industry/News.asp?Articleid=ArticleID6620031641.

Chapter 19: If It Walks like a Duck and Quacks like a Duck...

A fine article outlining some of the problems with bank wraps, some of which are also applicable generally to this type of account, is "Bank-Sold Wrap Accounts Don't Live Up to Sales Pitch," by Rob Carrick, *The Globe and Mail,* April 12, 2004. It is available at https://secure.globeadvisor.com/servlet/ ArticleNews/story/gam/20041204/STMAIN04.

You might also want to review an article by Kelly Rodgers, who wrote the following in an article appearing in *MoneySense,* June/July 2000:

> If you have $250,000 or more in your RRSPs and invest-
> ment account, your financial planner or stockbroker is
> likely to be extolling the virtues of wrap accounts. Should
> you listen? Well, that depends. In most cases, I think
> wrap accounts are the Ricky Martin of the investment
> world—superficially appealing but, in the end, much
> ado about nothing.

This article is available at http://www.rodgersinvestment consulting.com/Article9.asp.

I don't necessarily endorse Rodgers' comments about Mr. Martin's music, but I take her point about wrap funds!

I obtained the data concerning the actual and projected investments in wrap accounts from the March 2005 issue of *Investment Executive.* It is available at http://www.investment executive.com/client/en/News/DetailNews.asp?Id=27907&cat =22&IdSection=22&PageMem=&nbNews=&IdPub=113.

Chapter 20: Brokers Understand Fees but Not Risk

Harry Markowitz was awarded the 1990 Nobel Prize in Economics. He is the author of the book *Portfolio Selection: Efficient Diversification of Investments.*

Chapter 21: Too Many Stocks, Too Few Bonds

The seminal studies on the overwhelming importance of asset allocation in determining the variability of returns of a portfolio are: Gary P. Brinson, L. Randolph Hood, and Gilbert L. Beebower. "Determinants of Portfolio Performance." *Financial Analysts Journal,* vol. 42, no. 4, July/August 1986, 39–44; and Gary P. Brinson, Brian D. Singer, and Gilbert L. Beebower. "Determinants of Portfolio Performance II: An Update." *Financial Analysts Journal,* vol. 47, no. 3, May/June 1991, 40–48.

An excellent summary of some of the other studies on this subject can be found in an article entitled "Asset Allocation Revisited," co-authored by William E. O'Reilly and James L. Chandler, Jr., *Journal of Financial Planning,* January 2000.

Returns data comes from the Toronto Stock Exchange. The Canadian bond returns cited here are for the Broad Blended Composite Bond Index. The Canadian Equity return is the TSX 300 index.

The returns data for the S&P/TSX Composite Index and long-term Government of Canada bonds is set forth in *What Kind of an Investor Are You?,* Richard Deaves, Ph.D. Toronto: Insomniac Press, 2006 (p. 152).

For a discussion of why investment risk does not always decline over time, and why it is therefore not always true that younger investors should hold most of their portfolios in stocks, see an article entitled "The Fallacy of Time Diversification," available at: http://www.slcg.com/documents/Time_Diversification_-_September_30_2005.pdf.

This subject has been fully explored by a number of prominent economists who have persuasively debunked this myth. For example: Paul A. Samuelson. "Risk and Uncertainty: A Fallacy of Large Numbers." *The Collected Scientific Papers of Paul A. Samuelson,* ed. Joseph E. Stiglitz, Cambridge: MIT Press, 1966, 153–158; and Zvi Bodie. "On the Risk of Stocks in the Long Run." *Financial Analysts Journal,* May/June 1995, 18–22.

Chapter 23: Beware of House Funds!

The study comparing the poor performance of house funds with similar funds managed by independent fund families is based on data provided by Lipper, Inc., reported at http://money central.msn.com/content/p27026.asp.

Chapter 25: Beware of Hedge Funds!

In July 2003, the SEC estimated that hedge fund investments in the United States would reach over $1 trillion by the end of 2004. As of July 21, 2003, the SEC had instituted 46 cases involving hedge fund fraud, for a variety of unsavoury practices. See SEC Release No. IA-2266; File No. S7-30-04, available at http://www.sec.gov/rules/proposed/ia-2266.

The sorry tale of the fraud involving Portus Alternative Asset Management is exhaustively set forth on the website of the Ontario Securities Commission, at http://www.osc.gov. on.ca/HotTopics/Portus/portus_index.jsp.

The private study I did on the performance of Canadian hedge funds was done with the assistance of Sean Kelly, Kelly & Associates, West Palm Beach, Florida.

Extensive information for potential investors in hedge funds in Canada is set forth on the website of the Ontario Securities Commission at http://www.investored.ca/en/focus/ investmentproducts/ip_hedge_fund.htm.

The loose regulation of hedge funds in Canada is exacerbated by the loophole exploited by sellers of principal-protected notes (PPNs). PPNs permit investors who would otherwise not be permitted to invest in hedge funds to "get a piece of the action." However, it is the sellers of PPNs who are the prime beneficiaries, since the commissions are high and very difficult to discern.

For an article on the perils of PPNs, see "Hedge Hogs: Principal-Protected Notes Are All the Rage, but They Aren't Risk-Free," by Jeff Sanford, *Canadian Business Magazine,* January 16–29, 2006 issue, available at http://www.canadian business.com/markets/stocks/article.jsp?content=20060116_7 3581_73581&page=1#adSkip.

A very interesting article that describes in sobering terms the risks of Canadian hedge funds is "How Risky Are Hedge Funds?" by Levi Folk, February 26, 2004. Folk measured the "maximum draw down" of major hedge funds, which looks "at the worst possible loss an investor would have endured in a fund had he or she bought in at the worst possible time." The "maximum draw down" of the funds listed in this article ranged from a low of 29.68% to a high of 87.55%. The article is available at http://www.fundlibrary.com/features/rrsp/page.asp?id=11776&p_=y.

For a far rosier picture of the benefits of investing in Canadian hedge funds, see *Hedge Funds for Canadians, New Investment Strategies for Winning in Any Market,* by Peter Beck and Milos Nagy (John Wiley & Sons, 2006). The authors estimate the size of the hedge fund industry at the retail level in Canada at $16 billion.

The authors opine that less regulation of hedge funds is a good thing, because it "means more options, which in turn leads to potentially better performance."

Unfortunately, it can also increase the possibility of abuse.

It remains my view that the primary beneficiaries of hedge funds are the hedge fund managers. Ordinary investors would be well advised to avoid them.

The risks of jumping on the hedge fund bandwagon were recently set forth in a sobering report entitled "Statement of the Financial Economists Roundtable on Hedge Funds," signed by a distinguished group of economists after a round-table discussion held July 10 and 11, 2005, in Sonoma, California, under the auspices of the Stanford Graduate School of Business. In this statement, the economists noted, among many other risks and concerns, that the average life of a hedge fund is only "about three years."

The difficulty of evaluating the returns of hedge funds is discussed by Adel A. Al-Sharkas, in an article entitled "The Return in Hedge-Fund Strategies," *International Journal of Business,* 10(3), 2005, available at http://papers.ssrn.com/sol3/papers.cfm?abstract_id=778404

Professor Al-Sharkas cites Stefano Lavinio's *The Hedge Fund Handbook* (2000) as authority for the short shelf life of hedge funds.

An article in *The Washington Times* on February 28, 2005, entitled "The Bear's Lair: Instruments of Satan," stated, "It's very clear why ambitious hot-shot traders and speculators want to run hedge funds; what is not so clear is why anyone would invest in them." This article is available at http://www.accessmylibrary.com/comsite5/bin/pdinventory. pl?pdlanding=1&referid=2930&purchase_type=ITM&item_ id=0286-8443716.

A recent study evaluated the performance of 1917 hedge funds. The authors found that "the majority of hedge funds have not provided their investors with returns which they could not have generated themselves by mechanically trading S&P 500, T-bond and Eurodollar futures. Overall, only 17.7% of the funds studied beat the benchmark." (Harry M. Kat and Helder P. Palaro. "Superstars or Average Joes? A Replication-Based Performance Evaluation of 1917 Individual Hedge Funds." Alternative Investment Research Centre Working Paper No. 30, February 3, 2006. Available at http://ssrn.com/abstract=881105.)

I found this observation by the authors of this study to be particularly compelling:

In a way, it is quite surprising that so many people, on the buy-side as well as in academia, are so eager to believe that the, sometimes huge, alphas reported for hedge funds are truly there. Anyone who is well calibrated to the world we live in and the global capital markets in particular, knows how difficult it is to consistently beat the market, i.e., systematically obtain a better return than what would be fair given the risks taken. Over time, hundreds, if not thousands, of studies have confirmed this. Is it therefore likely that suddenly we are facing a whole new breed of super-managers; not one or two, but literally thousands of them? Of course not! And, if anything, the rise of the hedge fund industry has made global financial markets even more efficient, not less.

Chapter 27: Why Hasn't Anyone Told You?

For an informative discussion of the compensation of brokers, see "Reversal of Fortune: Compensation Trends 2002," at http://registeredrep.com/career/finance_reversal_fortune_compensation/index.html.

Information on the compensation of brokers in Canada was derived from Andrew Willis's article, "Except for Hedge Funds, the Street's Pay Looks Puny," globeandmail.com, May 16, 2003. It is available at http://www.globeadvisor.com/servlet/ArticleNews/story/gam/20030516/RANDY.

A helpful list of low-cost index funds available to Canadian investors may be found at: http://globefunddb.theglobeandmail.com/gishome/plsql/gis.process_fr?fr_param1=index&fr_mode=FUNDNAME&iaction=Go.

Chapter 30: Should Your Broker Act Only in Your Best Interest and Be Careful with Your Money?

The standard of care applicable to trustees in Canada is set forth as follows by the Supreme Court of Canada in Fales v. Wohlleben Estate, [1977] 2 S.C.R. 302, at 315:

> Traditionally, the standard of care and diligence required of a trustee in administering a trust is that of a man of ordinary prudence in managing his own affairs ... and traditionally the standard has applied equally to professional and non-professional trustees. The standard has been of general application and objective, though at times rigorous.

Chapter 31: Who Believes Me?

You can find a list (current only through June 30, 2001) of pension plans that seek market returns through index funds at www.ifa.com.

Dimensional Fund Advisors lists the names of some of its clients at http://www.dfaus.com/dimensional/clients.

The information concerning the amount of assets represented by index investments is from the speech by John Bogle referred to in the notes to Chapter 2.

The study demonstrating the decline of stock picking in the United States is Utpal Bhattacharya and Neal E. Galpin's "Is Stock Picking Declining Around the World?" (November 2005), available at http://ssrn.com/abstract=849627.

Chapter 36: Step 3: Select Your Investments

The information on the benefits to Canadian investors of owning foreign stocks was derived from an excellent chart entitled "A Balancing Act: Risk vs. Reward," available at http://mutualfunds.yahoo.ca/funds/invest.html.

Chapter 38: What About Income Trusts?

An extensive analysis of income trusts may be found in an article by Dirk Zetzsche, Ph.D, entitled "The Need for Regulating Income Trusts: A Bubble Theory," *University of Toronto Faculty of Law Review,* vol. 63, no. 1, 2005.

I also recommend an article by Vijay Log and Liping Want, entitled "The Growth of Income Trusts in Canada and the Economic Consequences," *Canadian Tax Journal,* vol. 52, no. 3, 2004.

My private study of income trusts was done with Sean Kelly, Kelly & Associates, West Palm Beach, Florida.

Chapter 40: Where Are the Pension Plans for Smart Investors?

I derived information concerning the basic principles underlying the investment choices in pension and RRSP plans, and related information about these plans, from an article by Ronald B. Davis, Associate Professor of U.B.C., Faculty of Law, entitled "The Enron Pension Jigsaw: Assembling

Accountable Corporate Governance by Fiduciaries," *University of British Columbia Law Review,* vol. 36, August 2003.

Chapter 41: Have the Inmates Taken Over the Asylum?

Professor Miller's observations about regulation benefiting the industry are set forth in a book written by him, entitled *Merton Miller on Derivatives* (New York: John Wiley & Sons, Inc., 1997, p. 45).

In an article reviewing a book by Mary G. Condon, entitled *Making Disclosure: Ideas and Interests in Canadian Securities Regulation* (Toronto: University of Toronto Press, 1998), Christopher C. Nicholls of the Dalhousie Law School, states:

> However, for me at least, when she attempts to illustrate her thesis with specific examples drawn from the early history of Ontario securities regulation, I am not always convinced that she has, in every case, successfully demonstrated the superiority of her model over some form of capture theory.

The "capture theory," in the context of securities regulation, asserts that regulation develops to accommodate the interests of the securities industry.

Appendix A
Asset Allocation Questionnaire

This questionnaire will help guide you to a proper asset allocation for your retirement portfolio. This is only meant to be a guide. For each individual investor, there are many factors that cannot possibly be addressed in a generic questionnaire.

STEP 1: Add up all of the money that you currently have saved for retirement. This should include RRSP plans or any other accounts you are using to save for retirement. Write this number down here:

Current Retirement Savings _____ A

STEP 2: What are your annual living expenses?

Annual Living Expenses _____ B

STEP 3: At what annual rate do you expect your salary to grow for the foreseeable future?

Annual Salary Growth Rate _____ C

STEP 4: How much are you contributing (in dollars) to retirement plans or any other accounts you are planning to use for retirement? Include your contributions to all retirement plans and also include any matching contributions from your employer.

Annual Retirement Contributions _____ D

STEP 5: Ratio of Current Retirement Savings to Annual Living Expenses

Divide the figure in Step 1 by the figure in Step 2. For example, if you have $250,000 currently saved for retirement and your living expenses are $50,000, this ratio would be 5.

$$\frac{\text{Current Retirement Savings (A)}}{\text{Annual Living Expenses (B)}} = \underline{\hspace{4cm}}$$

STEP 6: Figure out how many years you have until retirement. For example, if you are 55 and plan to retire at 70, you have 15 years until retirement.

Years Until Retirement = _____

STEP 7: Savings-Age Score (SAS)

On the matrix on page 173, find the intersection of your years to retirement (found in the far left column) and your ratio of current retirement savings to annual living expenses (found across the top). Identify the number in this cell. This is your "Savings-Age Score" (SAS). To continue the example, if your ratio of current retirement savings to annual living expenses was 5 and you plan to retire in 15 years, your SAS would be 30.

SAS SCORE = _____

How many years before retirement?	Ratio of current retirement savings to annual living expenses											
	<1	1-2	2-4	4-6	6-8	8-10	10-12	12-14	14-16	16-18	18-20	>20
41 to 45 years	80	78	72	60	40	28	20	12	8	4	2	0
36 to 40 years	76	74	68	57	38	27	19	11	8	4	2	0
31 to 35 years	72	71	65	54	36	25	18	11	7	4	1	0
26 to 30 years	68	67	61	51	34	24	17	10	7	3	1	0
21 to 25 years	56	55	50	42	28	20	14	8	6	3	1	0
16 to 20 years	48	47	43	36	24	17	12	7	5	2	1	0
11 to 15 years	40	39	36	30	20	14	10	6	4	2	1	0
8 to 10 years	24	24	22	18	12	8	6	4	2	1	0	0
1 to 5 years	16	16	14	12	8	6	4	2	2	1	0	0
Retired	8	8	7	6	4	3	2	1	1	0	0	0

STEP 8: RATIO OF ANNUAL RETIREMENT CONTRIBUTIONS TO ANNUAL LIVING EXPENSES

Divide the figure in Step 4 by the figure in Step 2. For example, if you contribute $5,000 per year to your RRSP Plan (the $5,000 includes your employer's matching contributions) and your annual living expenses were $50,000, this number would be 10%.

$$\frac{\text{Annual Retirement Contributions (D)}}{\text{Annual Living Expenses (B)}} = \underline{\hspace{3cm}}$$

STEP 9: GCS

On the matrix below, find the intersection of your annual salary growth rate (found in the far left column) and your ratio of annual retirement contributions to annual living expenses (found across the top). Identify the number in this cell. This is your "Growth-Contribution Score (GCS)."

GCS SCORE = _____

Annual growth of current salary	Ratio of annual retirement contributions to annual living expenses								
	0%	1–3%	3–5%	5–8%	8–10%	10–15%	15–20%	20–25%	>25%
8%+	15	15	14	11	8	5	4	2	2
5%–8%	14	14	13	11	7	5	4	2	1
3%–5%	14	13	12	10	7	5	3	2	1
1%–3%	13	12	11	10	6	4	3	2	1
0%–1%	11	10	9	8	5	4	3	2	1
0%	9	9	8	7	5	3	2	1	1

STEP 10: Risk Assessment Score (RAS)

Answer the following 10 questions. Next to each answer for every question, there is a number. When you decide which answer is right for you, make note of the number next to the answer. Once you have finished all of the questions, you will add up these numbers. All of these numbers added together will give you your Risk Assessment Score (RAS). Enter this score on page 178.

1. In addition to your long-term investments, approximately how many months of your current expenses do you have set aside in cash or money market funds for unexpected needs?

A. 6 months... 3

B. 4 months... 2

C. 2 months... 1

D. None 0

2. How many years have you been investing in the stock market?

A. None 0

B. Less than 1 year................................. 1

C. More than 1 year but less than 5 years.............. 2

D. More than 5 but less than 10 years................. 3

E. 10 years or more 4

3. I consider myself to be knowledgeable about investments and financial matters.

A. Strongly Agree................................... 4

B. Agree.. 3

C. Somewhat Agree................................. 2

D. Disagree 1

E. Strongly Disagree 0

4. How do you feel about this statement?

I want my investments to be risk-free.

Note: Investments with no risk have little or no expected return beyond the rate of inflation.

A. Strongly Agree 0

B. Agree. 0

C. Somewhat Agree 1

D. Disagree 3

E. Strongly Disagree 4

5. I am willing to expose my investment portfolio to some degree of risk in order to increase the likelihood of higher returns.

A. Strongly Agree 4

B. Agree. 3

C. Somewhat Agree 2

D. Disagree 0

E. Strongly Disagree 0

6. I am comfortable with a portion of my portfolio being invested internationally.

A. Strongly Agree 4

B. Agree. 3

C. Somewhat Agree 2

D. Disagree 1

E. Strongly Disagree 0

7. When my investment portfolio declines, I begin to think about selling off some of my positions and reinvesting at some later date.

A. Strongly Agree 0

B. Agree. 1

C. Somewhat Agree 2

D. Disagree 3

E. Strongly Disagree 4

8. Some investors hold portfolios that consist entirely of stocks. Such investors lost approximately 20 percent of their portfolios in October 1987. If you owned a risky investment that fell by 20 percent over a very short period, what would you do?

A. Sell all the remaining investment 0

B. Sell 75% of the remaining investment 0

C. Sell 50% of the remaining investment 1

D. Sell 25% of the remaining investment 2

E. Hold on to the investment 4

9. What is the worst 12-month percentage loss you would tolerate for your long-term investments, beyond which you would sell some or all of your investment?

A. 24% 4

B. 16% 3

C. 12% 2

D. 8% 1

E. Zero; any loss is unacceptable to me 0

10. Based on $100,000 invested since 1975, the following choices show the highest 12-month gain and the highest 12-month loss of five different index portfolios. Which portfolio would you choose?

Note: The portfolios with the widest range between the loss and the gain also have higher average returns.

A. Loss of $560; Gain of $23,500 0

B. Loss of $5,100; Gain of $31,000 1

C. Loss of $10,500; Gain of $42,700 2

D.   Loss of $15,700; Gain of $51,600 3

E.   Loss of $22,200; Gain of $63,100 4

RAS SCORE =

STEP 11: PORTFOLIO ALLOCATION SCORE (PAS)
[SAS + GCS + RAS]

Add your Savings-Age Score (SAS), your Growth-Contribution Score (GCS) and your Risk Assessment Score (RAS). This number is your Portfolio Allocation Score (PAS). Find where your score lies in the distribution below. The matrix below gives you a range for the stock portion of your allocation. Your recommended percentage allocated to stocks in most cases would be in this range. Once you choose the percentage allocation to stocks, the remainder will be invested in bonds.

PAS SCORE = _____

% Stocks		
PAS	Upper Boundary	Lower Boundary
80–120	90	70
70–79	80	60
60–69	70	50
50–59	60	40
40–49	50	30
30–39	40	20
20–29	30	10
10–19	20	0
0–9	10	0

Appendix B
Risk and Return Summary

All performance data are expressed in percentages and are hypothetical investment results over the period 1977–2005.

	Low Risk	Medium-Low Risk	Medium-High Risk	High Risk
	20/80	40/60	60/40	80/20
Average annual return (Geometric)	10.14%	10.89%	11.56%	12.15%
Annualized standard deviation	7.51%	8.47%	10.25%	12.51%
Worst single calendar year	−2.07%	−2.02%	−7.99%	−13.95%
Worst two-calendar-year period	7.59%	−2.71%	−12.51%	−21.80%
Worst three-calendar-year period	13.32%	0.37%	−12.74%	−24.69%

Composition of model portfolios:

20/80
    2%   iShares CDN Composite Index Fund (XIC)
   10%   iShares CDN S&P 500 Index Fund (XSP)
    8%   iShares CDN MSCI EAFE Index Fund (XIN)
   80%   iShares CDN Bond Index Fund (XBB)

40/60
    4%   iShares CDN Composite Index Fund (XIC)
   20%   iShares CDN S&P 500 Index Fund (XSP)
   16%   iShares CDN MSCI EAFE Index Fund (XIN)
   60%   iShares CDN Bond Index Fund (XBB)

60/40
    6%   iShares CDN Composite Index Fund (XIC)
   30%   iShares CDN S&P 500 Index Fund (XSP)
   24%   iShares CDN MSCI EAFE Index Fund (XIN)
   40%   iShares CDN Bond Index Fund (XBB)

80/20
    8%   iShares CDN Composite Index Fund (XIC)
   40%   iShares CDN S&P 500 Index Fund (XSP)
   32%   iShares CDN MSCI EAFE Index Fund (XIN)
   20%   iShares CDN Bond Index Fund (XBB)

Raw data used to produce performance numbers:

iShares CDN Composite Index Fund (XIC) = actual fund returns 2002–2005,
(TSX 300 Index–0.25% per year) 1977–2001

iShares CDN S&P 500 Index Fund (XSP) = actual fund returns 2002–2005,
(S&P 500 return in US dollars adjusted for US/Canadian currency
exchange rate–0.15% per year) 1977–2001

iShares CDN MSCI EAFE Index Fund (XIN) = actual fund returns 2002–2005,
(MSCI EAFE return in US dollars adjusted for US/Canadian currency
exchange rate–0.50% per year) 1977–2001

iShares CDN Bond Index Fund (XBB) = actual fund returns 2002–2005,
(TSX Blended Broad Composite Bond Index Index–0.30% per year)
1990–2001, (Lehman Brothers World Bond Index–0.30% per year)
1977–1989

Additional Resources

A number of excellent books explore the subjects discussed in this book in far more detail than I have here. The problem I have with some of them is that they provide so much information that the overall message tends to get lost and cause investors to throw their hands up in collective despair. Unfortunately, the place they turn to for assistance is—you guessed it—the local hyperactive broker or advisor, who is only too pleased to "assist."

Nevertheless, for those who want to delve deeper, here are some of the best resources:

Richard Deaves, Ph.D. *What Kind of an Investor Are You?* Toronto: Insomniac Press, 2006.

John De Goey. *The Professional Financial Advisor: Ethics, Unbundling and Other Things to Ask Your Financial Advisor About.* Toronto: Insomniac Press, 2004.

Ted Cadsby. *The Power of Index Funds: Canada's Best-Kept Investment Secret.* Distributed by General Distribution Services, 1999.

Burton Malkiel. *A Random Walk Down Wall Street.* New York: W.W. Norton & Company, 8th edition, 2006.

Mark T. Hebner. *Index Funds: The 12-Step Program for Active Investors.* Newport Beach, CA: IFA Publishing, 2005.

John Bogle. *Bogle on Mutual Funds.* New York: McGraw-Hill, 1993.

William Bernstein. *The Four Pillars of Investing.* New York: McGraw-Hill, 2002.

Larry Swedroe. *The Only Guide to a Winning Investment Strategy You'll Ever Need.* New York: St. Martin's Press, 2005.

David F. Swensen. *Unconventional Success: A Fundamental Approach to Personal Investment.* New York: Free Press, 2005.

The website of Index Funds Advisors, www.ifa.com, is the pre-eminent source on the internet for the most exhaustive information and research on the subject matter of this book. I highly recommend it.

Acknowledgments

It takes a village to write a book and this book is no exception.

I benefitted greatly from the insights of Andrea Crozier, my editor at Penguin Canada.

Carol Mann, of the Carol Mann Agency, believed in this book and was a wonderful source of encouragement and support.

Edward S. O'Neal, Ph.D., an assistant professor of finance at the Babcock Graduate School of Mangement, Wake Forest University, helped me understand and explain the more technical aspects of finance.

Rajeeva Sinha, Ph.D., professor of finance, Odette School of Business, University of Windsor, was kind enough to review the manuscript and provide me with his valuable insights.

Sean Kelly, of Kelly & Associates, was of great assistance to me in performing a number of private studies.

Mark T. Hebner graciously gave me permission to use many of the quotations in the book, which are among those that can be found at Mark's stellar website, www.ifa.com.

Sabrina Weill, a talented author herself, was a source of meaningful guidance and advice.

Mandy and Andrew Solin spent countless hours assisting with design issues and providing much needed perspective.

My wife, Patricia Solin, read and reread the text, and made a significant contribution to the final product.

Index